Contents

Woodlands

Jewelry Designs
from Nature

woodlands, gardens, sea

Heather Powers

Dear Patty -
Find inspiration
in the everyday!
- Heather Powers

KALMBACH BOOKS

Kalmbach Books
21027 Crossroads Circle
Waukesha, Wisconsin 53186
www.Kalmbach.com/Books

Project photography by Kalmbach Books.
Step-by-step and inspiration photography by author, Heather Powers.

Published in 2011
15 14 13 12 11   1 2 3 4 5

Manufactured in the United States of America

ISBN: 978-0-87116-428-5

Edited by Karin Van Voorhees
Art Direction by Lisa Bergman

Publisher's Cataloging-in-Publication Data

Powers, Heather.
   Jewelry designs from nature : woodlands, gardens, sea / Heather Powers.

   p. : ill. (chiefly col.) ; cm.

   ISBN: 978-0-87116-428-5

   1. Jewelry making—Handbooks, manuals, etc. 2. Beadwork—Handbooks, manuals, etc. I. Title.

TT212 .P68 2011
739.274

Gardens

Sea

Introduction

If nature is the teacher, there will always be a new lesson.

I'm not alone in finding inspiration from the beauty of nature. From poets to painters, designers to musicians, nature has inspired the creative process through the ages. Whether it is majestic and infinite like the stars and oceans, or the most delicate detail of gossamer wings or a spider's web, we stand in awe of nature's design.

My own personal inspiration from nature comes from many sources: through the filter of Van Gogh's paintbrush, words penned by Emily Dickinson, a photograph framed by a skilled eye, or a design found in a piece of fabric. Each designer, artist, or writer shares such inspiration. I find that my memories and joy from experiencing nature anew all mix into my jewelry designs. I've never met a creative block that couldn't be overcome from a walk in the woods or stroll near a lake.

The designs in this book are inspired by my childhood in the forests of Michigan, of tall evergreens and oaks. They are inspired by fields of wildflowers, dragonflies skimming over ponds, and gardens kept by faithful hands. They are inspired by my trips to the ocean and days spent with my feet in the water. They are inspired by treasures of sea-worn glass and shells washed upon the shore. My work comes from these memories and experiences. My jewelry is more than just adding a bead to a string; each piece speaks to me of the wonders in the world. It tells a story of how we can be amazed and inspired every day if we open our eyes, unplug, and turn our hearts toward the living world around us.

Heather Power

How to Use this Book

I hope you will find this book very friendly and easy to use. I'd like to call a few things to your attention before you begin to help you make the most of the information contained here.

Project introductions explain my design philosophy and will help you make choices if you'd like to substitute beads.

Read the materials lists carefully. I've been as specific as I can. Of course, you may substitute beads of similar size and shape. I've specified chain and wire lengths in the materials list, and those should be pre-cut before you start working.

These projects use simple tools as described on p. 13. Most only use chainnose pliers, roundnose pliers, and wire cutters.

The step-by-step instructions with photos explain specific techniques or how to make unique components. Start here and make any components first.

The large annotated photo is a road map to help you combine components, beads, and basic techniques to finish the jewelry. Many projects are finished with chain and it may not show in the photo, but it is explained in the directions.

Simple techniques are explained in Basics, beginning on p. 88. The Basics Summary accompanying each project gives you an idea of the skills you'll need to know before you begin.

Walk with me now, through woodlands and gardens and on ocean shores as I share my inspiration and design ideas.

Art Beads

Each project in this book features beads created by artists; these mini-masterpieces are called art beads. I've found that many beadmakers are inspired by their surroundings, and there is no shortage of art beads that celebrate nature and its splendor. Artists create with clay, glass, and metal as they explore the colors, textures, and design principles borrowed from Mother Nature. It's my hope that you'll learn a few new techniques, find inspiration, and use these designs as a springboard for your own creativity. As you gather together materials, don't worry if you can't find the exact bead I've used. Finding something that fits your taste and style will help make your creation even more personal and rewarding.

Where to Find Art Beads You can buy art beads directly from artists online or at bead shows. Check with your local bead store to see if they carry handmade beads. Etsy, an online marketplace, is a fun place to shop for artisan beads. You can also read more about art beads on my blog, *artbeadscene.com.*

A

B

C

D

Clay: Ceramic, Porcelain, Raku, and Polymer

Ceramics is a general term used for fired clay items. Different types of clay offer different sensibilities to beads. **Earthenware (A)** beads are glazed with paints and chemicals to achieve a variety of colors and finishes. They can be full of detail if made from ornate molds or sculpted by hand and rustic. **Porcelain (B)** is a finer clay that takes more skill to work with. You'll find that porcelain beads feel lighter than their earthenware cousins. Porcelain beads are white underneath and can offer brighter colors. **Raku (C)** is a firing process that uses fire and smoke to create incredible organic finishes, often in iridescent colors and with crackle textures. Raku beads and pendants are best left for necklaces and earrings. The firing process can produce beads that are porous and may not withstand wear on a bracelet. **Polymer clay (D)** is a man-made clay created from a plastic known as polymer. This is a low-fire clay that is durable and lightweight. Artists use a wide variety of techniques to create beads with colorful clay: from painting, transferring images, stamping, sculpting, and creating designs with canes. Polymer clay is a chameleon that can mimic a range of materials. You'll find polymer beads that are matte and natural looking, buffed and polished to a high gloss, and everything in between.

Glass: Lampworked, Enamel, and Boro

Lampworkers take rods of glass and use a torch to melt the glass around a wire or bead mandrel. Beads can be created in numerous designs as beadmakers dance with the flame. Lampworked beads can be simple designs using crushed glass, known as frit. They can use only one or two colors in small spacer beads. Or, they can be masterfully designed feats of glass engineering that take hours to produce. Lampworked beads come in a surprising number of textures ranging from etched matte glass and bumpy frit designs to perfectly smooth and shiny beads. Examples of lampworked beads are shown in the first two columns, at right. **Enamel** is glass melted onto a metal surface. These can found in a variety of components, pendants, and beads, usually on copper or brass bases. The first bead in the third column is enameled. **Boro** beads are lampworked beads created from borosilicate glass that was originally used for cookware and laboratory glass. These beads are extremely hard and durable. The glass produces amazing organic colors and designs. The last three beads in the third column are boro beads.

Metal: Pewter, Bronze, Shibuichi, and Metal Clay

Most **metal** beads use a lost-wax casting method. Beadmakers cast a mold from a small sculpted piece or from found objects. You'll find designers casting beads in **pewter**, **bronze**, or an alloy of mixed metals. **Sterling silver** beads contain 92.5 percent silver mixed with 7.5 percent copper while **shibuichi** beads are made from a mixture of 75 percent silver and 25 percent copper. **Metal clay** in silver, copper, or bronze can be fashioned like regular clay into any shape or design and is fired in a kiln. Beads pictured (clockwise from top right) are made from sterling silver, bronze, sterling silver metal clay, shibuichi, and pewter.

Collage: Paper on Wood and Metal

These art beads are created using images printed on paper and applied to either a wooden base or a metal bezel. They are then coated with a protective finish on the wood bases or the bezels are filled with **resin**, a plastic-like material that hardens to a crystal-clear shine.

Supporting Cast

I like to choose materials that support my earthy and natural sensibility. I don't mind a dyed or enhanced stone, but if you choose them, be aware their color may change over time. I'm more likely to choose a material for its immediate beauty rather than an intrinsic value. I am more than happy to forgo a cultured pearl when a freshwater one offers such delightful organic textures and color.

Gemstones (A)—Gemstones can be found in a wide range of cuts, colors, and styles. I like to look for stones that have faceted cuts or offer unusual textures or colors. Handpick strands of stones whenever possible for the best color and quality. Some stones are dyed or enhanced and the color may change over time. If this is important to you, shop with a trusted vendor who can answer questions about the stones.

Pearls (B)—The luminescent quality of freshwater pearls adds depth to any design. Pearls have smaller holes than most beads; use them with thinner gauges of wire, headpins, or beading wire. Use a bead reamer to enlarge too-small holes. Colorful pearls are usually dyed.

Wood (C)—Wooden beads add warmth and rich color. Some wooden beads have larger holes and you may need to add spacers into a design to cover them.

Resin (D)—A plastic-like material in a range of soft matte colors, resin can double as faux beach glass or add a touch of glowing color to a floral design.

Glass (E)—Czech glass beads, molded into leaves and flowers, are among my favorite picks for nature-inspired creations. I also love adding small touches of sparkle with crystal or fire-polished glass. Recycled glass beads are tumbled to a matte finish.

Glass seed beads (F)—Glass seed beads come in so many colors and shapes, it can be overwhelming. One thing to keep in mind about seed beads is the larger the number, the smaller the bead. Size 8º seed beads are great spacers. Size 11º is the most common size; these beads can be strung, used with wire, or stitched into beadwork with needle and thread. Delicas are smaller than 11ºs and are a uniform cylinder shape. I also love using peanut seed beads that look like a double seed bead with a hole in the middle. Seed beads can be found in metallic, silver-lined, transparent, and opaque finishes.

Metal seed beads (G)—These are the only accent beads I can't live without. These tiny seed beads are made from real metal and add the perfect touch as spacers or metallic design elements. They also can be used for clasps and at the end of fringe. Pick antique copper to go with copper and brass. Nickel seed beads match sterling silver, pewter, or gunmetal findings.

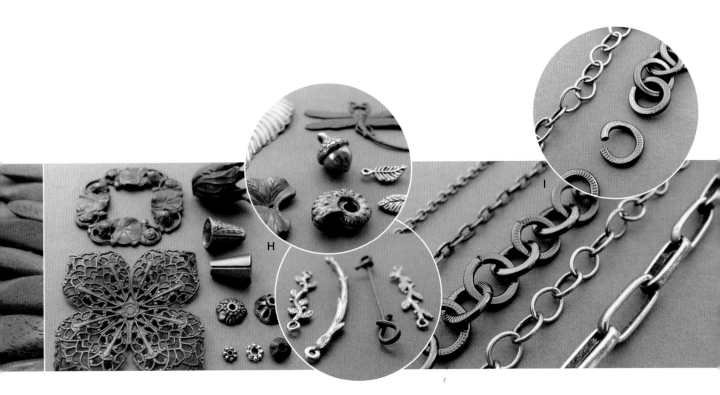

Metal beads and findings (H)—Made from pure metal, such as sterling silver or copper, metal alloys (base metals), or as plated finish over brass or copper, metal beads can be found in a shiny raw state, antiqued to a dark finish, or even painted. Metal beads used in this book include pendants, charms, and beads. I love mixing metal connectors with chain and beads for both design purposes and to fill in a large area on a necklace. Filigree can be used to wrap beads or make pendants. Bead caps can be used in between beads or as beads themselves.

Chain (I)—Chain can add color, texture, and structure to a design. Chain will either have soldered (closed) links or open links. Open-link chain can be substituted for jump rings. Simply remove one link from the chain to add into a design.

Wire (J)—To understand wire sizes, remember the smaller the number, the thicker the wire. A 16- or 18-gauge wire is thick and can be used for clasps or sturdy links. A finer-gauge wire like 22- or 24-gauge is used with smaller hole beads or for delicate wirework. Silver wire can be purchased as dead soft or half-hard. Soft wire is appropriate for larger gauges or if you plan to use a ball peen hammer to harden it once it's been formed. The

silver wire used in this book as links, clasps, or connectors is half-hard. This half-hard wire doesn't bend as easily and works better for structural items. Copper and brass wire can be found at your local hardware store and offers an affordable alternative to sterling silver. Colored copper wire in an antique brass finish matches perfectly with antiqued brass findings. Be aware that the copper can show once the wire is cut. Make sure to tuck the ends of the wire on wrapped loops so the copper doesn't show.

Beading wire (K)—I use 19- or 49-strand flexible beading wire in .014–.019 diameters. This bundled steel wire, coated with plastic, can be found in silver, copper, or brass colors to match your findings. The .014 wire is thinner and holds less weight; use this wire for pearls, seed beads, wood, and other lightweight materials. The .018–.019 wires are heavier and hold stones, glass, and other heavy beads.

Fireline beading thread—This single-ply thread is made from spun and bonded polyethylene fibers. It's extremely strong and it doesn't stretch, making it ideal for bead-stitching projects.

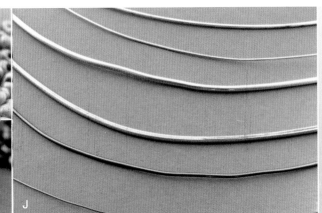

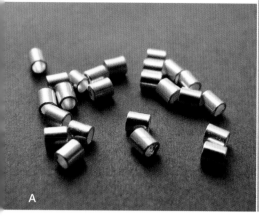

Crimp beads (A)—For all of my stringing projects I use 2 mm crimp tubes. They fold over into a nearly invisible element in a jewelry piece and offer a secure connection for clasps.

Clasps (B)—A few of my favorite clasp styles include the toggle and hook and eye. Most of my clasps are artist's creations or ornate findings that are part of the design. You can make your own clasps, like the wire one in the Birch Forest Bracelet on p. 22, or create one from unexpected elements, like the Coral & Shell Necklace on p. 80.

Jump rings (C)—Jump rings are the workhorses of jewelry designers and so vital to almost every design in this book. Use small jump rings for a seamless connection or large ones as part of chain. Etched jump rings add texture and strength to a design.

Earring wires, eyepins, and headpins (D)—Earring wires such as lever backs, fish hooks, or kidney wires offer a variety of commercial solutions for quick and easy earrings. Eyepins have a loop on one end and save time when creating links. Headpins can have either a flat end or a ball end. I use 1-, 2-, and 3-in. headpins and stock up on these in silver, gunmetal, copper, and brass.

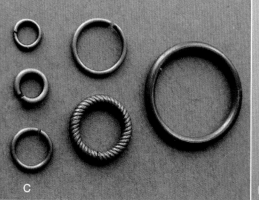

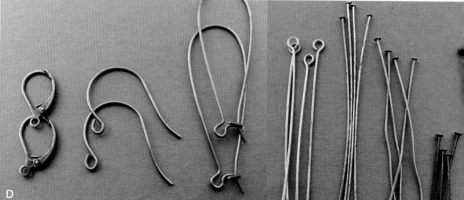

Tools of the Trade

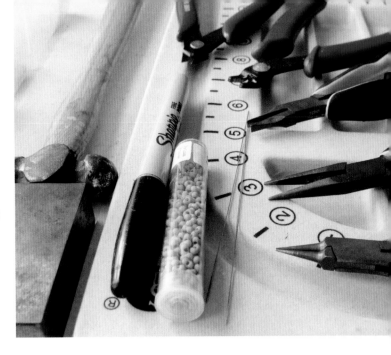

I like to keep things simple and low-tech when it comes to jewelry tools. I use the most basic of tools for the projects in this book. I prefer Lindstrom pliers and recommend that you buy the best pliers you can afford. Ergonomically designed pliers are easier on your hands, and higher quality tools help produce professional results by not marring wires.

Chainnose pliers—These pliers have a flat, smooth surface. Use them to open and close jump rings and earring wires, and to tighten wrapped loops. You'll need two pairs of pliers to close jump rings. I use two chainnose pliers, but you could also add bentnose pliers to your tool box.

Bentnose pliers—Similar to chainnose pliers, the ends or these pliers are bent at an angle to give more flexibility.

Roundnose pliers—Roundnose pliers have a graduated jaw and are used to create loops of various sizes including links, loops, tendrils, and clasps.

Wire cutters—Flush cutters are flat on the outside and create a flat cut on wire. Use these to cut beading wire in stringing projects and to trim metal wire.

Crimping pliers—Crimping pliers have a series of grooves that fold and close crimp tubes. Using crimping pliers creates secure closures for necklaces and bracelets.

Bench block and ball peen hammer— If you are new to jewelry making, you may not have one yet, but be brave and add it. You'll love the way you can texture components or flatten wire to give it more strength. A bench block is flat steel block. Place the wire or metal on the block and hammer it. A ball peen hammer has a flat side for flattening and a rounded side that makes a dappled texture. (A folded hand towel under the block muffles the hammering sound.)

Mandrels—I like to use what I have on hand to shape larger loops in my wirework. I used a tube of beads or a large permanent marker for most of the large links in the projects. You also may use a dowel or a ring mandrel.

Beading needles—For the projects in this book I use a big-eye needle that has a opening down the center. This long needle allows for passes through several larger beads.

G-S Hypo cement—Use this glue on knots when working with seed beads and Fireline beading thread.

Bead board or bead mat—No need to get fancy; you can use anything that will keep your beads from rolling onto the floor. A bead board has grooves to hold the beads and measurements along the sides. I use bead boards most often so that I don't have to hunt for a measuring tape. A bead board also can be helpful for planning out an asymmetrical design, since laying out your project before you assemble the pieces can help you see parts of the design that may need work. Place a bead mat inside a tray to store projects for later.

Lighting—I rarely use special lights in my studio because natural light is abundant. A task light may help during seed bead projects. It can be frustrating to work with tiny beads if you can't see them properly. I recommend a full-spectrum task light to help see colors clearly and to avoid the glare you can get from regular desk lamps.

A Note about Storage

Bead storage could be a book unto itself. I wish I had advice for taming an ever-growing bead stash, but mine likes to creep across the studio and take over any flat surface available. I would say whatever works best for you is the system to use. For most beginners and for some of us old pros, the divided storage containers are a quick and easy answer. I separate my gemstone beads by color, and then materials such as crystals, glass, and wood have their own containers, along with a container or two for each type of metal for my findings. I stack these trays on a shelf under my work desk and have them labeled on the outside for quick reference.

I find it hard to tuck my art beads away into these storage containers though. I love seeing them on my work desk, and I like to fill little trays or tiny bowls with some of my favorite treasures. Seeing them on display will often inspire a new creation.

Woodlands

if my
words
had
wings

I find inspiration in the pattern made by branches swaying above my head as I walk through the forest. I find inspiration in the world of birds: their remarkable eggs and nests. I find inspiration in the crunch of snow in the winter, and the summer sun dappling through the trees; the songs of birds in spring, and autumn's splendor of colorful leaves. Nature puts on a show and the wooded forest is one of its beloved theaters.

Evergreen
Bracelet

Mary Harding ceramic toggle,
Green Girl Studios pewter owl

supplies

- 19 mm pewter owl
- **12** 20 mm stick pearls
- **4** 12 mm faceted rutilated quartz beads
- **10** 4 mm copper heishi beads
- 2 g green 11º seed beads
- **8** copper 11º seed beads
- 38 mm ceramic toggle clasp
- **2** 2 mm copper crimp tubes
- **4** links of copper chain
- **3** 4 mm copper jump rings
- 2 ft. (61 cm) 24-gauge brass colored wire
- flexible beading wire

finished length: 7½ in. (19.1 cm)

basics

- attach a clasp
- make an entwined loop
- make a folded crimp

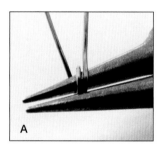

A

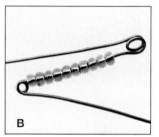

B

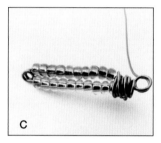

C

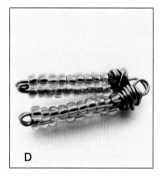

D

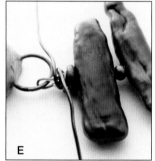

E

F

Pine needle components

A, B, C, D Cut a 4-in. length of wire. Wrap the center twice around roundnose pliers. String 10 green seed beads on one side. Wrap both wires around the pliers to form a loop. String 10 green seed beads on the other side. Wire-wrap around the loop with the remaining wire. Make four needle components.

Finishing

E, F Wire-wrap over the crimp beads as in an entwined loop.

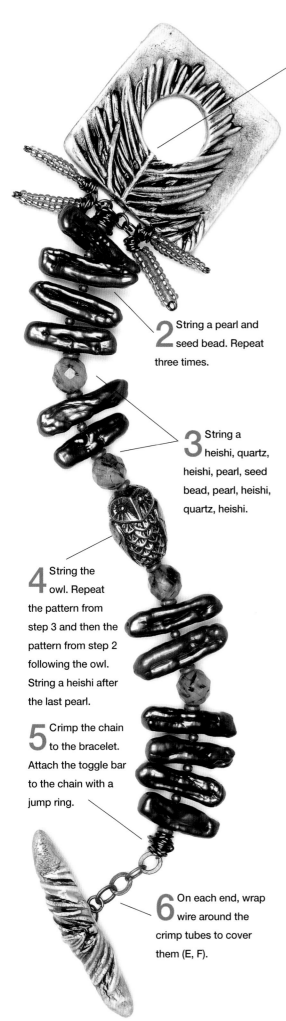

1 Crimp the large part of the toggle to the beading wire. Attach the wire pine-needle components to each side of the clasp loop with jump rings. String a heishi.

2 String a pearl and seed bead. Repeat three times.

3 String a heishi, quartz, heishi, pearl, seed bead, pearl, heishi, quartz, heishi.

4 String the owl. Repeat the pattern from step 3 and then the pattern from step 2 following the owl. String a heishi after the last pearl.

5 Crimp the chain to the bracelet. Attach the toggle bar to the chain with a jump ring.

6 On each end, wrap wire around the crimp tubes to cover them (E, F).

Bonus Earrings

supplies

- **4** 12 mm pewter leaf charms
- **2** 12 mm ceramic bead caps
- **2** 12 mm polymer clay disks
- **2** 4 mm copper heishi beads
- **2** 12 mm faceted rutilated quartz beads
- **2** 2-in. brass eyepins
- pair of brass earring wires

1 Open the eyepin and attach two pewter leaves; close the eyepin.

2 String a bead cap, polymer clay bead, heishi, and quartz bead. Make a loop. Attach an earring wire.

3 Make a second earring.

Inspired by the realism of the spruce bough ceramic toggle, I created a wire and seed bead fringe to mimic the pine needles. The pearls were picked not only for their shape, which adds a twig-effect to the design, but for their size. They offer a visual balance to the hefty toggle. Even the rutilated quartz beads have inclusions that look like pine needles. The pewter owl at the back of the bracelet works as a counter-weight for the toggle. A clasp this stunning is worn on top of the wrist.

Nurture Thy Soul Necklace

Humblebeads clasp,
Cindy Gimbrone lampworked headpin,
Elemental Adornments bird

supplies

- 18 mm silver bird bead
- **3** 8 mm brown button pearls
- **3** 6 mm faceted teal pearls
- **3** 6 mm Indian pink AB crystals
- 25 mm polymer clay toggle clasp
- 3 in. (7.6 cm) double-dipped headpin
- ¾ in. (1.9 cm) 2 mm copper cable chain
- **2** 4-link sections 15 mm patina chain
- 7¼ in. (18.4 cm) 9 mm ring/connector copper chain
- **3** 2½-in. (6.4 cm) 24-gauge wire copper ball headpins
- **11** 3 mm copper jump rings
- 6 in. (15 cm) brass-color 24-gauge wire cut into three 2-in. (5 cm) lengths
- 9 in. (23 cm) patinated copper 22-gauge wire cut into three 2-in. lengths and one 3-in. length

finished length: 19 in. (48 cm)

basics

- open and close jump rings
- make an entwined loop
- make a tendril

A

B

C

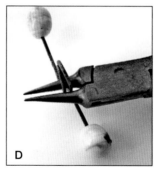

D

A Make three wrapped links with brass wire and brown pearls. Connect the links with jump rings.
B Make three wrapped links with the patinated copper wire and crystals.
C Create three tendril wrapped dangles with the teal pearls and copper ball headpins.
D Make the headpin toggle bar: Grasp the double-dipped headpin in the center with roundnose pliers and make a double loop.

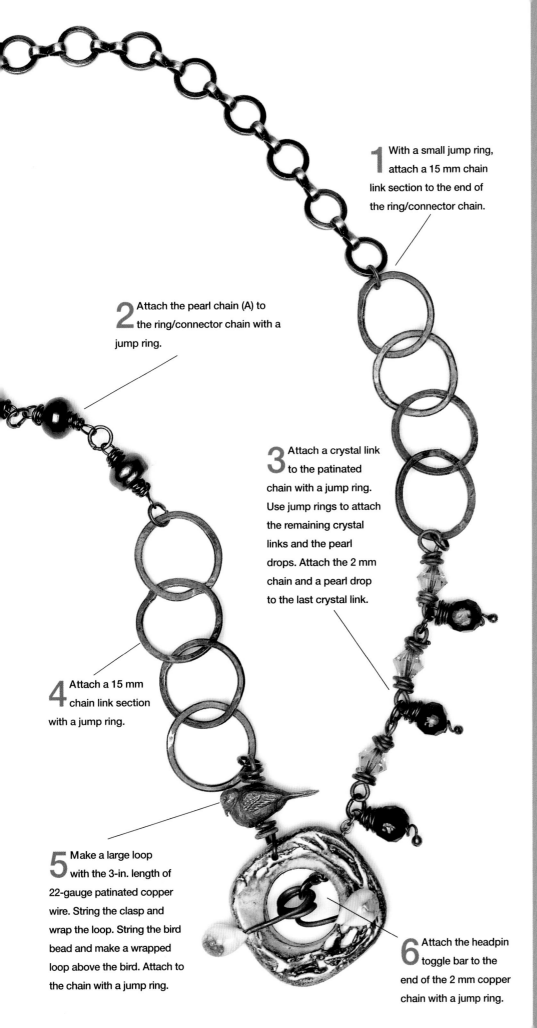

1 With a small jump ring, attach a 15 mm chain link section to the end of the ring/connector chain.

2 Attach the pearl chain (A) to the ring/connector chain with a jump ring.

3 Attach a crystal link to the patinated chain with a jump ring. Use jump rings to attach the remaining crystal links and the pearl drops. Attach the 2 mm chain and a pearl drop to the last crystal link.

4 Attach a 15 mm chain link section with a jump ring.

5 Make a large loop with the 3-in. length of 22-gauge patinated copper wire. String the clasp and wrap the loop. String the bird bead and make a wrapped loop above the bird. Attach to the chain with a jump ring.

6 Attach the headpin toggle bar to the end of the 2 mm copper chain with a jump ring.

I used repetition to pull together this eclectic collection of chain and beaded links to accent a handcrafted toggle. I paired a large patinated copper chain with a smaller chain, both of them repeating the circular shape in the toggle clasp. A tiny silver bird perches on the nest, and both she and the crystals are wrapped in patinated copper wire. It's a subtle touch that adds to the rustic quality of the necklace. To juxtapose the earthy feel, I used delicate pink crystals and tiny head-pins shaped into tendrils on the pearl dangles. The toggle clasp was fashioned out of a double-dipped lampworked headpin. The ends look like little eggs and add the perfect touch to the clasp.

Out on a Limb
Necklace

Jade Scott copper and resin components,
Green Girl Studios pewter beads,
Humblebeads polymer clay beads

supplies

- 45 mm copper and resin branch pendant
- 45 mm copper and resin branch connector
- 38 mm polymer clay birch bark bead
- 26 mm pewter raven bead
- 15 mm pewter bell drop pendant
- **4** 12 mm polymer clay willow disks
- 12 mm faceted aventurine rondelle
- 8 mm jasper rondelle
- **3** 7 mm Czech glass flowers
- **3** 10 mm copper beadcaps
- 1½-in. (3.8 cm) copper leaf-fringe chain
- 3 in. (7.6 cm) brass box chain cut into two 1½-in. lengths
- 7 in. (18 cm) brass oval and circle link chain cut into one 3½-in. (8.9 cm) length and one 4-in. (10 cm) length
- **9** 7 mm oval copper jump rings
- 20 mm copper magnetic flower clasp
- **3** 2-in. (5 cm) copper ball headpins
- 22-gauge brass-colored wire

finished length: 18½ in. (47 cm) with a 4-in. (10 cm) dangle

basics

- open and close jump rings
- entwined loop

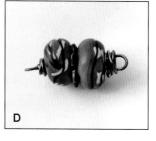

A Cut a 3-in. length of wire. Make a wrapped loop and string a beadcap (dome down), an aventurine rondelle, and a disk bead. Make a wrapped loop above the beads.

B Make a wire-wrapped link with the birch bead.

C String a flower bead on a balled headpin and make a wrapped loop above the bead. Repeat for a total of three.

D Make a wire-wrapped link with a disk bead, a flattened bead cap, and a disk bead.

To complete the necklace, attach the brass and oval chain length to each side by opening and closing a link.

E On each side, open an end link of chain and attach the clasp. Close the link.

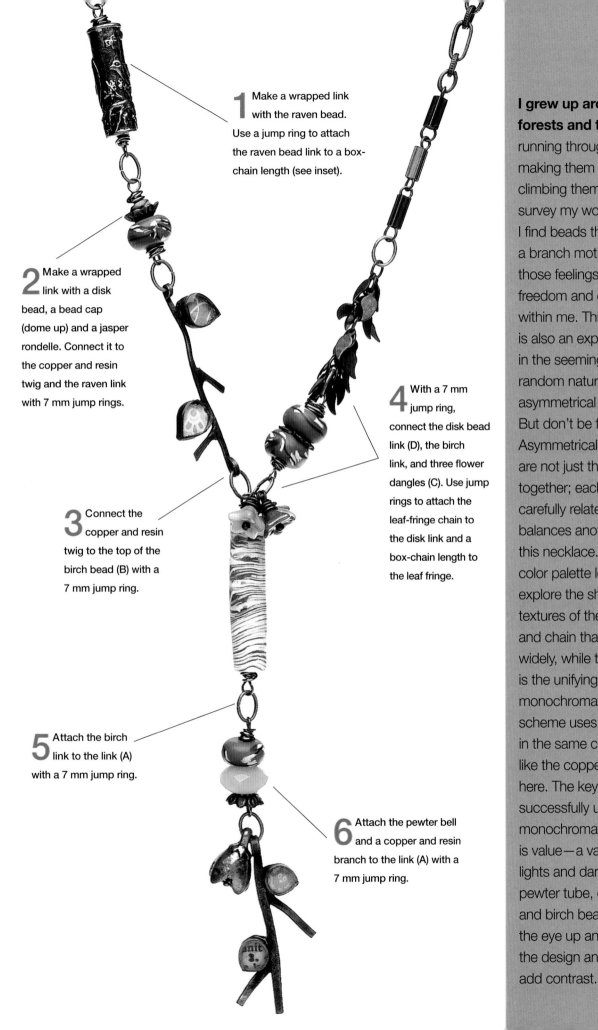

1 Make a wrapped link with the raven bead. Use a jump ring to attach the raven bead link to a box-chain length (see inset).

2 Make a wrapped link with a disk bead, a bead cap (dome up) and a jasper rondelle. Connect it to the copper and resin twig and the raven link with 7 mm jump rings.

3 Connect the copper and resin twig to the top of the birch bead (B) with a 7 mm jump ring.

4 With a 7 mm jump ring, connect the disk bead link (D), the birch link, and three flower dangles (C). Use jump rings to attach the leaf-fringe chain to the disk link and a box-chain length to the leaf fringe.

5 Attach the birch link to the link (A) with a 7 mm jump ring.

6 Attach the pewter bell and a copper and resin branch to the link (A) with a 7 mm jump ring.

I grew up around forests and trees: running through them, making them into forts, climbing them to survey my world. When I find beads that have a branch motif, it stirs those feelings of freedom and exploration within me. This necklace is also an exploration in the seemingly random nature of asymmetrical design. But don't be fooled. Asymmetrical designs are not just thrown together; each piece carefully relates to and balances another part of this necklace. A limited color palette lets the eye explore the shapes and textures of the beads and chain that vary widely, while the color is the unifying factor. A monochromatic color scheme uses colors in the same color family, like the copper palette here. The key to successfully using monochromatic colors is value—a variation in lights and darks. The pewter tube, charm, and birch bead draw the eye up and down the design and add contrast.

Birch Forest
Bracelet

Sue Beads lampworked disks

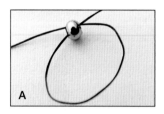 A

 B

 C

 D

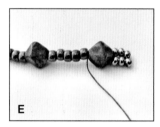 E

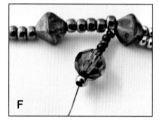 F

 G

 H

 I

supplies

- **8** 14 mm lampworked disk beads
- **25** 8º bronze glass seed beads
- **2 g** 11º purple glass seed beads
- **42** 11º nickel seed beads
- **6** 6 mm glass bicone beads
- **11** 6 mm silver flat spacer beads with larger holes
- **30** accent beads: 6 each of 5 different beads or charms in various sizes
- **12 mm** pewter pinecone charm
- **15 mm** pewter leaf charm
- **3 mm** jump ring
- **6 in. (15 cm)** half-hard 20-gauge sterling silver wire
- Fireline 6 lb. test
- beading needle

finished length: 8 in. (20 cm)

basics
- open and close jump rings
- hook and eye clasp

A, B, C Thread the needle with a long length of beading thread. Pick up an 11º nickel seed bead and sew through it again to secure. Pick up five nickel seed beads and sew through to create a loop. Begin Step 1.

D Pick up a pattern of a 6 mm glass bead and five 8º seed beads until there are six 6 mm glass beads strung. Pick up a flat spacer bead.

E Pick up six 8º seed beads and sew back through the flat spacer and 6 mm glass bead.

F Pick up five 11º purple seed beads, an accent bead, and a nickel seed bead.

G Sew back through the accent bead, skipping the nickel bead. Pick up five 11º purple seed beads and sew through the next 6 mm glass bead. The beadwork will form a little triangle. Repeat this process of making the fringe using the same accent bead until you've reached the disk beads.

Sew through the disk beads and the nickel-bead loop at the end, and sew back through the disk beads.

Sewing toward the other end, repeat the process of making fringe using a new type of accent bead at the end of each fringe. When you reach the end, sew through the nickel bead loop and repeat the process until there are six different accent beads in each fringe cluster.

Knot and tie off the thread, tuck in loose ends, and trim excess threads.

Make the clasp

H Cut two 3-in. (7.6 cm) lengths of sterling silver wire. On one length, string a spacer, a disk bead, and a spacer and make a wrapped link. Connect the link to the disk end of the bracelet before finishing the wraps.

I Use the remaining 3-in. wire to create a hook clasp, stringing it through the beaded loop before finishing the wraps.

1 Make a loop (A–C). Pick up a repeating pattern of a spacer and disk bead seven times. Pick up a spacer.

2 Follow D, E, F, G to make a 7-in. (18 cm) bracelet.

3 Attach the pinecone and leaf charm to the hook with a jump ring.

Don't Be Afraid of Seed Beads

If you have never tackled a bead-stitching project—one with seed beads and thread—do not be overwhelmed! If you can sew on a button, you can create the fringe elements needed for both of the stitching projects in this book. Yes, it's as simple as sewing on a button. With just a little practice and patience, you will find a brand new world opened to your jewelry design opportunities.

Here are a few pointers for working with seed beads:

- Don't try to pick up the seed beads with your fingers and put them on the needle. Press your needle through the center of a seed bead and tilt the needle to pick up the bead. Pick up several and then let them slide down the thread.

- Have good lighting. It's hard to work with seed beads if you can't see the holes.

- Work slowly and steadily. If a knot develops in your thread, don't give up. Most knots can be undone with just a little patience.

- Secure your work—tie the ends of the thread tightly and weave them back through several beads before cutting your thread. Use a dab of beading glue to secure knots.

- Work in a clear area—it can be frustrating when threads catch onto tools or other items on your bead table.

- Don't tackle a project that requires counting if you are going to be distracted. Wait until you have some quiet time to avoid losing count and getting frustrated.

If you aren't ready for a bead stitching project, use seed beads for texture in your strung designs as shown in several other projects in this book.

Create this asymmetrical bracelet inspired by the colors and textures of a wintery forest. The bracelet mixes a sundry collection of beads in the fringe. The disk beads mirror the fringe clusters and create an interesting contrast between the fluid movement of the beaded fringe and the curve of the disk beads. Choose the accent beads from colors in the art beads so that the two sections of the bracelet visually play back and forth.

The Sweetest Song Necklace

Erin Siegel ceramic leaf, Green Girl Studios shibuichi and pewter, Elaine Ray ceramic rounds, Jubilee ceramic houses, Humblebeads polymer clay, C-Koop enameled clasp

supplies

- 55 mm painted brass leaf pendant
- 46 mm ceramic leaf
- 32 mm shibuichi bird pendant
- 22 mm filigree brass ring
- 20 mm polymer clay egg
- **2** 15 mm ceramic house beads
- 14 mm pewter nest bead
- **4** 14 mm polymer clay disks
- **2** 12 mm ceramic round beads
- 15 mm enameled magnetic clasp
- **14** 6 mm silver flat spacers
- **5** 10 mm brass jump rings
- **8** 3 mm jump rings
- 2-in. (5 cm) brass eyepin
- 37-in. (.94 m) 3 mm gunmetal curb chain, cut into four 9¼-in. (23 cm) lengths
- 4–5 ft. (1.2–1.5 m) 20-gauge brass-colored wire

finished length: 22½ in. (57.2 cm) with a 4¾ in. (12.1 cm) dangle

basics

- entwined loops and links
- opening and closing jump rings

A

B

C

D

E

F

Create the pendant

A, B, C String the egg bead onto 3–5-in. (7.6–13 cm) of wire. Make an entwined loop above the egg. Make a large loop at the bottom of the egg and wrap the loop. Continue wrapping the loop around the base of the egg to form a nest.

D, E, F Cut a 5-in. length of wire and make an entwined loop at one end. String a spacer, a disk, and a spacer and make an entwined loop above the beads. Repeat with the round beads. Repeat with the house beads, but just use one spacer at the bottom of the house. Make a total of four disk, two round, and two house wrapped links.

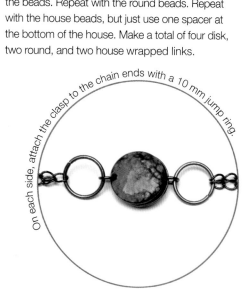

On each side, attach the clasp to the chain ends with a 10 mm jump ring.

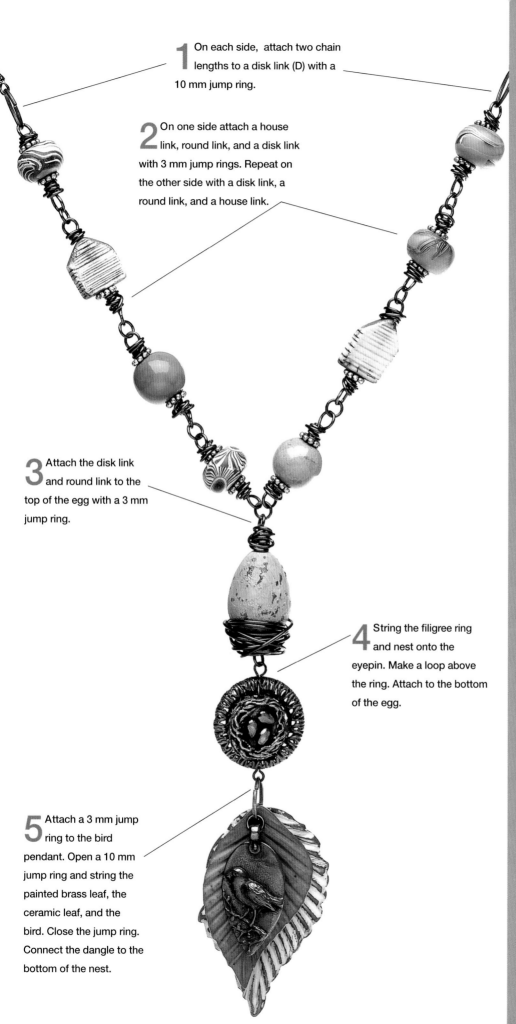

1 On each side, attach two chain lengths to a disk link (D) with a 10 mm jump ring.

2 On one side attach a house link, round link, and a disk link with 3 mm jump rings. Repeat on the other side with a disk link, a round link, and a house link.

3 Attach the disk link and round link to the top of the egg with a 3 mm jump ring.

4 String the filigree ring and nest onto the eyepin. Make a loop above the ring. Attach to the bottom of the egg.

5 Attach a 3 mm jump ring to the bird pendant. Open a 10 mm jump ring and string the painted brass leaf, the ceramic leaf, and the bird. Close the jump ring. Connect the dangle to the bottom of the nest.

Layering three similarly shaped pendants makes a dramatic focal. I created a wire nest for the egg and repeated the tangled wire loops on each of the bead links to unify the necklace with the pendant. Silver mixed with brass provides a crisp accent to the muted color palette.

Above the Treetops Necklace

Green Girl Studios shibuichi and pewter,
Humblebeads polymer clay

A

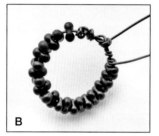

B

C

D

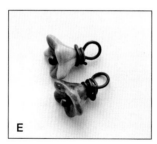

E

F

G

supplies

- 35 mm shibuichi bird toggle clasp
- **15** 15 mm faceted smoky quartz ovals
- **6** 14 mm polymer clay disks
- **12** 10 mm copper beadcaps
- **6** 7 mm copper melon beads
- **12** 7 mm Czech glass flowers
- **5 g** 2 x 4 mm Japanese peanut seed beads
- **10** copper 11º metal seed beads
- **12** 2-in. (5 cm) brass ball headpins
- **8** 15 mm brass jump rings
- **2** 10 mm brass jump rings
- **2** 2 mm copper crimp tubes
- **2** links of 2 mm brass cable chain
- 7 mm jump ring
- **2** 8-in. (20 cm) lengths 22-gauge brass colored wire
- 22 in. (56 cm) beading wire

**finished length:
  23 in. (58 cm)**

basics

- entwined loops and links
- opening and closing jump rings
- crimping

A, B, C Make a large loop with the brass wire by shaping it around a tube of beads or a permanent marker. String 21 seed beads onto the loop and wire wrap the ends to form a ring. Overwrap the wire to form a stronger link. Make two beaded links.

D Make a wire-wrapped link with a bead cap, disk bead and bead cap. Face the bead caps away from the disk bead. Make six.

E Make a wire-wrapped dangle with a flower on a ball headpin. Make 12 flower dangles.

F On the beading wire, string a crimp tube and the jump ring. Go back through the crimp tube and crimp.

G Attach the bar (bird) of the clasp and the chain links with a 5 mm jump ring.

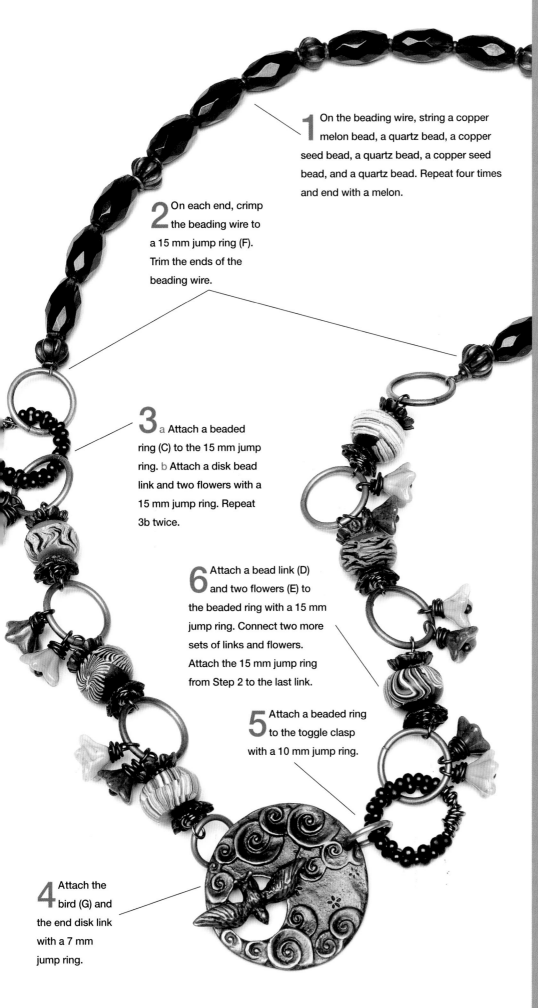

1 On the beading wire, string a copper melon bead, a quartz bead, a copper seed bead, a quartz bead, a copper seed bead, and a quartz bead. Repeat four times and end with a melon.

2 On each end, crimp the beading wire to a 15 mm jump ring (F). Trim the ends of the beading wire.

3 a Attach a beaded ring (C) to the 15 mm jump ring. b Attach a disk bead link and two flowers with a 15 mm jump ring. Repeat 3b twice.

6 Attach a bead link (D) and two flowers (E) to the beaded ring with a 15 mm jump ring. Connect two more sets of links and flowers. Attach the 15 mm jump ring from Step 2 to the last link.

5 Attach a beaded ring to the toggle clasp with a 10 mm jump ring.

4 Attach the bird (G) and the end disk link with a 7 mm jump ring.

Artist-made toggle clasps are meant to be displayed front and center, like this little bird that is soaring over clouds. I took my cues for this design from the color of the metal in the clasp. Shibuichi is an ancient Japanese technique of mixing copper and silver together to create a metal that is warm and mysterious. Repeating the elements in the brass jump rings and beaded wire elements add a lightness to the necklace that is offset by faceted smoky quartz. The effect: a bird soaring above the treetops of a dark forest.

Be True
Necklace

Heather Wynn polymer clay, Green Girl Studios pewter

supplies

- 45 mm polymer clay pendant
- 30 mm pewter feather pendant
- 20 mm pewter bird charm
- 29 mm brass filigree ring
- **2** 25 mm lepidolite faceted marquis beads
- 12 mm glass bead
- **3** 10 x 6 mm faceted glass rondelles
- **7** 6 mm round faceted crystal beads
- a variety of beads for beaded rings:

     19 3 mm fire-polished glass beads

     36 4 mm labradorite faceted rondelles

     38 nickel 11º seed beads

     15 copper 11º seed beads

     28 4.5 mm keishi pearls

     8 6 x 4 mm pearls

     16 glass 8º seed beads
- 6 mm smoky quartz round
- 20 mm brass ring
- 25 mm brass pod toggle bar
- 4 mm silver flat spacer
- **4** 15 mm brass jump rings
- 6 mm silver jump ring
- 6 mm brass jump ring
- **8** 2 mm silver crimp tubes
- 1¾ in. (4.4 cm) 8 mm brass cable chain
- 36 in. (.9 m) 22-gauge sterling silver half-hard wire, cut into one 5-in. (13 cm), three 4-in. (10 cm), three 2½-in. (6.4 cm) , and four 3-in.(7.6 cm) lengths
- 30 in. (76 cm) beading wire cut into seven 4-in. and one 2-in. (5 cm) length

finished length: 19½ in. (49.5 cm)

A

B

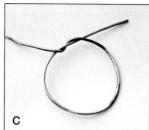

C

D

Technique: Beaded Rings

A, B String beads and a crimp tube onto a piece of beading wire. Go through the crimp tube with each end of the beading wire from opposite sides; go through several additional beads on each side. Pull the wire tight to form a circle and crimp the crimp tube. Trim the wire ends.

Make rings in the following patterns (do not crimp the crimp tubes until you link the rings into the necklace, shown at right):
a. alternate 11 3 mm glass beads with copper
b. alternate 7 glass beads with nickel seed beads
c. 28 nickel seed beads
d. 16 8º glass seed beads
e. alternate six labradorite beads with nickel seed beads
f. eight oval pearls
g. 28 keishi pearls with nickel seed beads on each end
h. five labradorite beads and one copper seed bead (repeat four times)
i. 16 labradorite beads with a silver seed bead on each end

Technique: Wire Rings

C, D Wrap a length of wire around a tube of beads or large marker to form a large circle. Wrap both ends of the wire around the ring to form a secure connection. Hammer the ring.

Make two 12 mm and one 20 mm wire rings.

Technique: Large-loop Link

E With a length of wire, form an oversized loop around a bead tube or marker, and then make the first half of a wrapped loop. String a bead, and make the first half of a wrapped loop on the other end. Hammer the loops. Complete the wraps as you build the necklace, pictured at right.

Make a large-loop link with:
j. a 10 mm faceted glass bead and 5 in. of wire.

Make standard-size loop links with:
k. a 10 mm faceted glass bead and 3 in. of wire
l. a 10 mm faceted glass bead and 3 in. of wire

E

m. a lepidolite marquis and 4 in. of wire (make two)
n. a 12 mm glass bead and 3 in. of wire
o. a 6 mm quartz round and 3 in. of wire

1 Connect beaded rings as shown, crimping after the connection is made. Attach the three-ring chain to the filigree ring with a 15 mm jump ring.

2 Use a beaded link (o) to connect the hammered ring and the cable chain. Use a marquis link (m) to connect the chain and the small wire ring (D). On the other side, connect link (k) to the end beaded ring and to link (j). Connect link (j) to link (l) and beaded ring (a).

3 String a flat spacer and the bird onto a 2½ in. (6.4 cm) piece of wire. Center the beads and make a wrapped loop. Open the brass jump ring and connect the bird to the filigree ring. Close the jump ring.

4 Attach a marquis link (m) to a wire ring (D) and the filigree ring. Complete the wraps.

5 Attach a 6 mm jump ring to the feather pendant. Use a 15 mm brass jump ring to link the feather pendant, the wire ring (D) from Step 2, and the labradorite ring (i). Use the glass link (n) to connect the labradorite ring and the pearl ring.

The secret message "to thine own self be true," found on the back of the feather, is the inspiration for this necklace. I paired the pendant with some feathered friends to symbolize freedom; I wanted to give the whole necklace a feeling of movement and openness. I wrapped the wire links to look like twigs. The beaded ring links are a fun way to create connectors in a design that uses many circular elements, while the marquis beads, pendants, and toggle bar add linear qualities to the design. Each part of the design relates to another.

6 Connect the pearl ring (f) and a wire ring (D) and crimp the pearl ring.

... with 3 mm beads and close. Attach the toggle and the ring with a 6 mm silver jump ring.

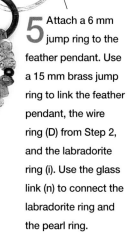

7 Crimp the labradorite ring (e). With a 15 mm brass jump ring, attach the labradorite ring, the pendant, and the pearl ring.

basics
- wrapped loops and links
- opening and closing jump rings
- crimping

Note: See p. 71 for detailed directions for filling the toggle pod.

Three Sisters
Necklace

Block Party Press polymer clay

supplies

- 28 x 35 mm polymer clay pendant
- **5** 25 mm silver branch connectors
- **5** 8 mm faceted rutilated quartz rondelles
- **7** 6 mm yellow jade rounds
- **7** 1-in. (2.5 cm) silver headpins
- 45 mm silver hook and eye leaf clasp
- 8-in. (20 cm) 8 mm silver oval chain
- **15** 8 mm silver oval jump rings
- 20-in. (51 cm) sterling silver 22-gauge half-hard wire, cut into five 4-in. (10 cm) lengths

finished length: 21 in. (53 cm)

basics

- plain loop
- opening and closing a jump ring

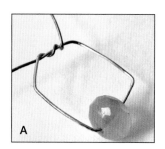
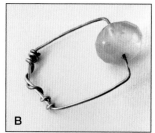
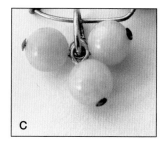

Create links and dangles

A, B Make a 45-degree bend in a length of wire with chainnose pliers. String a quartz bead onto the wire. Leave a ½-in. (1.3 cm) space and make another 45-degree bend. Repeat on the other side of the wire. This creates a house shape. Wrap the ends of the wire around the top of the house to form a secure link. Make five beaded links.

C Make seven beaded dangles with the 6 mm beads and headpins.

D Detail of clasp and dangle connection.

Wear the chain across the back of the neck so the clasp shows in the front.

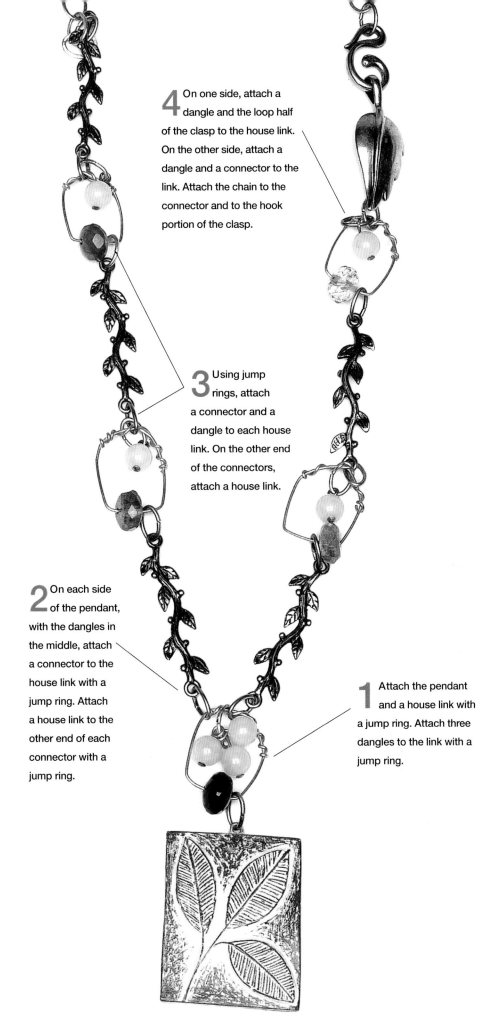

4 On one side, attach a dangle and the loop half of the clasp to the house link. On the other side, attach a dangle and a connector to the link. Attach the chain to the connector and to the hook portion of the clasp.

3 Using jump rings, attach a connector and a dangle to each house link. On the other end of the connectors, attach a house link.

2 On each side of the pendant, with the dangles in the middle, attach a connector to the house link with a jump ring. Attach a house link to the other end of each connector with a jump ring.

1 Attach the pendant and a house link with a jump ring. Attach three dangles to the link with a jump ring.

This pendant was named "Three Sisters" by the bead artist. My mom and her two sisters came to mind when I began designing this necklace. Layers of meaning went into the design: wire links have a slight house shape to represent home and family; the subdued color palette takes its cue from the focal bead and symbolizes the quiet strength of the ties that bind sisters; and the leaf motif is repeated in the details of the connectors and the leaf-hook clasp. Each part speaks to the other in this combination that is light and airy, like leaves swaying on branches and the laughter of sisters.

Autumn Lariat

River Art Glass lampworked acorns,
Skully B Beads lampworked ruffles

supplies

- 35 mm lampworked acorn
- 22 mm lampworked acorn
- **2** 15 mm lampworked ruffled beads
- **4** 7 mm labradorite faceted rondelles
- **6** 7 mm pyrite rounds
- **6** 6 mm red crystal bicones
- **10** 4 mm copper flat spacers
- **6** 14 mm brass filigree cones
- **2** 10 mm brass etched jump rings
- **16** 4 mm brass jump rings
- **8** 2-in. (5 cm) brass eyepins
- 19½-in. (49.5 cm) brass oval link chain cut into one 11½-in. (29.2 cm) length and eight 1-in. (2.5 cm) lengths

finished length: 32 in. (81 cm)

basics

- plain loop links
- opening and closing jump rings

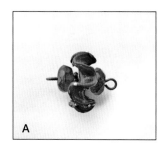

A

B

Create links

A On an eyepin, string a labradorite bead, a flat spacer, a lampworked ruffle bead, a flat spacer, and a labradorite bead. Make a loop above the beads. Make two links.

B On an eyepin, string a pyrite bead, a crystal, a filigree cone, and a flat spacer. Make a loop above the beads. Make six links.

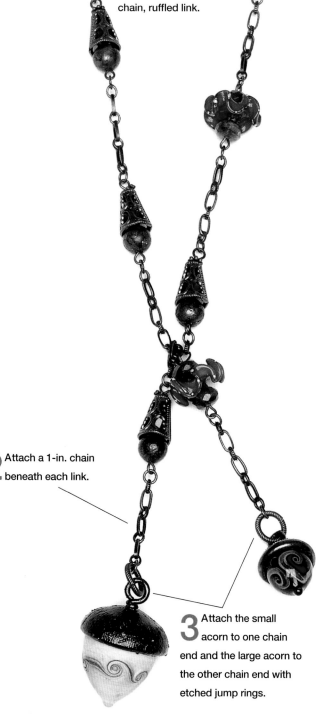

1 Attach a cone link to each end of the 11½ in. (29.2 cm) chain with a 4 mm jump ring. Attach a 1-in (2.5 cm) chain length to each cone link. On one end, attach a ruffled link , chain, cone link, chain, cone link. On the other side, attach cone link, chain, cone link, chain, ruffled link.

2 Attach a 1-in. chain beneath each link.

3 Attach the small acorn to one chain end and the large acorn to the other chain end with etched jump rings.

Variation

Create a mod-inspired variation of this lariat with lampworked beads from German glass artist Dora Schubert. Pair with a brass leaf blank and brass fern charm at the ends. Simple brass cones mixed with blue and yellow crystal beads offer a more mid-century vibe.

Lariat means rope in Spanish, and it's a fun style for showing off art beads that are begging to be noticed! These acorns were created from real acorn caps electroplated in copper. I alternated chain with coordinating beaded links. The chain is wrapped over itself to form a secure closure, and the weight of the acorns keeps the lariat from untying. Do you see the red bicones peeking from the filigree cones? They take their cue from the ruffled lampworked beads, just as the pyrite and labradorite beads reflect the color of the acorns' designs. The overall design is influenced by the Arts and Crafts movement that was so heavily inspired by the natural world.

Winter Solstice
Necklace

Lynn Davis pewter pendant

4 On each end, string 22 6 mm beads.

supplies

- 25 mm pewter deer pendant
- **39–40** 10–14 mm rutilated quartz teardrops
- **4** 8 mm smoky quartz coins
- **44** 6 mm pyrite rounds
- **4** 2 mm silver round beads
- 20 mm pewter toggle clasp
- **2** 2 mm silver crimp tubes
- 8 mm gunmetal brass jump ring
- flexible beading wire
- 2-in. (5 cm) 24-gauge sterling silver wire

finished length: 19 in. (48 cm)

basics

- bail loop
- opening and closing jump rings
- crimping
- attaching a clasp

Earrings

Bronze porcelain beads from Marsha Hedrick paired with textured rings and delicate leaf charms reflect the muted colors of the necklace.

1 Center a teardrop on the wire. Bend wire to form a bail and make a wrapped loop above the bail. Connect the dangle to the bottom of the pendant before completing the loop.

5 Attach a clasp to the ends of the necklace.

3 On each end, string 18–21 teardrops, a silver bead, two coins, and a silver bead.

2 Attach the jump ring to the pendant and center the pendant on the beading wire.

Design Note:

Because the gemstone teardrops vary in size, string an equal length (not necessarily an equal number) on each side of the focal pendant. Here, 21 are on the left and 18 are on the right, but both sections are 4 in. (10 cm) long.

Winter branches encapsulated in ice were the inspiration of this design. The rutilated quartz is a striking contrast to the simple pyrite beads that offer the look of the frozen ground of the forest floor. The small detail of smoky quartz coins offers a transition from the larger flat beads to the smaller rounds. The pendant is pewter cast from an antique button; its medieval appeal reminds me of ancient celebrations of the winter solstice.

Oh Nuts
Necklace

Diane Hawkey ceramic squirrel and acorn beads,
Earthenwood Studio ceramic disk bead and
acorn charm, Gaea ceramic acorn pendant,
Jade Scott copper and resin acorn pendant

supplies

- 28 mm ceramic squirrel bead
- 18 mm ceramic disk
- **3** 15–20 mm ceramic acorn beads
- 22 mm ceramic acorn charm
- 28 mm ceramic acorn pendant
- 25 mm copper and resin acorn pendant
- 27 in. (69 cm) 12 mm brass rolo chain
- 2 in. (5 cm) 5 mm brass link chain
- **3** 1-in. (2.5 cm) brass headpins
- 5¼-in. (13.3 cm) brass ball headpin or length of brass wire
- **1–3** 4 mm brass jump rings

finished length: 26 in. (66 cm) with a 4½ in. (4.5 cm) dangle

basics

- tendril wrapped loop
- entwined loop
- plain loop
- opening and closing jump rings

This close-up view of the squirrel bead shows the
tendril wrap at the bottom and the entwined loop
above. Tendril-wrapping the headpin balances the
size of the bead and reinforces the necklace's
woodland theme.

2 Make an acorn dangle by stringing an acorn bead on a headpin and making a loop above the bead. Make three, and attach to the chain dangle. Attach the ceramic pendant and other acorn to the bottom chain links by opening and closing the chain links (or use jump rings).
Use a jump ring to attach the copper acorn to the bottom of the necklace.

1 Make a tendril-wrapped loop at the end of the ball headpin or length of wire. Attach the 2-in. length of chain before closing and wrapping the loop. Add the disk bead and squirrel bead above the tendril. Make a wrapped loop above the bead and connect to each end of the 27-in. chain before completing the wraps.

Earrings

supplies

- **2** 15 mm acorn beads
- **2** links of chain from necklace
- **10** 2 x 4 mm peanut beads
- **2** balled headpins
- pair of earring wires

1 String an acorn bead on a headpin and make the first half of a wrapped loop above the bead.

2 Connect a chain link to the loop and complete the wraps.

3 String the dangle and five peanut beads onto the earring wire.

4 Make a second earring.

The amazing thing about artist-made beads is the creativity of the designers. Take a simple object like an acorn, ask five different beadmakers to create one, and you'll find five completely different beads. This necklace plays with that diversity by offering a treasure-trove of textures in the tassel-style pendant. Like a squirrel storing away nuts for winter, I gathered up an awesome collection of acorn beads to cluster together. To balance out the bulky pendant, I added a clean and bold brass oval chain.

Nature, Poetry, and Your Story: Discover Your Visual Language

I love reading poems inspired by nature; they speak to the essence of my soul. There are emotions and responses to nature that I don't have words for, but poets with an efficiency of language can sum up those moments with beauty and grace.

Can you create poetry with beads? Can you hint at a story or convey an emotion with your jewelry? Of course you can. Just as a poet uses words strung together to tell a story, you can use beads that have meaning to the wearer and weave a message with symbols.

Nature and poetry can be interpreted in two ways using beads. First, you can start with a poem and use the visual imagery to create a piece of jewelry.

I shall be telling this with a sigh
Somewhere ages and ages hence:
Two roads diverged in a wood, and I—
I took the one less traveled by,
And that has made all the difference.

—*Robert Frost*

Think of Frost's words, and how you could create a necklace that diverged into two paths: one wild and overgrown, and the other with a path trodden from previous travelers. You could make one side of the necklace wild with green and brown beads, mixed with wire components to represent tree branches. The other side could be simple and sparse with a heavy chain to balance out the wild path.

The Dickinson passage may be easier to interpret with birds, wings, or feather components that are suggested in the poem. One could create a bracelet featuring a bird charm and the word "hope" stamped onto a bead. Or you may find a bird bead and wire-wrap it on a brass branch, perched and waiting. The beads can hint to the story or speak to it directly.

The second way to translate nature and poetry into your jewelry is to use beads to create a story. You can choose each part of a design deliberately, playing with common symbols, colors, and textures to portray personal meaning. Read about the story behind my Leaving Home bracelet (p. 40) for an example of how I used beads as symbols to create a bracelet that was about more than beads strung together. Using symbols in objects and materials to add meaning to a design can introduce a hidden layer of poetry to your jewelry.

Two paths necklace

from the pages of
Heather's sketchbook

hope

Hope is the thing with feathers
That perches in the soul.

—Emily Dickinson

A Conversation with Mary Harding— Mary Harding Jewelry

Mary is a ceramic bead artist who creates with clay and objects from the earth. She uses multiple glazes and stains to produce organic effects. Mary's pendants and toggles make me feel like I've taken a nature walk and walked away with some of the best treasures offered by the forest and fields.

Q. Your work often incorporates impressions from actual objects from nature. Do you go out hunting for these treasures? Or do you find them in your everyday experiences and know they will make a great bead design?

A. I don't actually go out hunting because I live in a giant pasture, so to speak, which is full of wildflowers and weeds that are beautiful. I just pick plants I like and try them out. They do not all work out. I am often surprised by what works out really well. Sometimes it is the least likely plant, like the burdock or the lilac seeds or the thistle leaf. I often don't use the plant in its entirety because a part of it is so much better looking to me.

Q. Do you keep a journal of ideas and inspirations from nature or is your work more immediate?

A. I don't keep a journal at all except for my blog which is a sort of journal. I don't ever plan out a piece before I see how it looks in clay; it never seems to work the other way for me. Once I see the plant in the clay, then I do try different angles or pieces of it for the finished piece. Some-times I make a list of what clay I want to use, or if I want to make beads or pendants or toggle clasps for a specific studio session so I can stay focused. Whether or not I stick to the list is another matter. Often I will see something in what I am working on that is much more exciting to me and that is what ends up happening.

Leaving Home Bracelet

Green Girl Studios pewter clasp, Diane Hawkey ceramic word bead, Jubilee ceramic house bead, Cindy Craig lampworked beads

Clasped, the bird sits on the nest.

1 Crimp the nest part of the clasp to the beading wire.

2 String a spacer, a lampworked disk, a spacer, and five wooden beads.

3 String a seed bead, a house, a spacer, a lampworked disk, a spacer, a word bead, a spacer, six wooden beads, and four seed beads.

4 Crimp the bird end of the clasp to the beading wire (A).

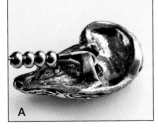

A Close-up view of crimp at bird-toggle end.

supplies

- **11** 25 mm wooden beads
- 24 mm ceramic word bead
- 20 mm ceramic house bead
- **2** 15 mm lampworked disks
- **5** 3 mm silver flat spacers
- **5** nickel 11º seed beads
- 30 mm pewter bird nest clasp
- flexible beading wire

finished length:
   7½ in. (19.1 cm)

basics

- crimping
- attach a clasp

When creating this design, I let the materials come together to tell a story. The clasp is a bird in the nest; the bird is the toggle portion of the clasp. I paired it up with wooden beads to symbolize trees. But something happens when you go beyond picking a bead for the color or size. I choose beads to say something—by using a word bead that says "grow," I allude to something of a story in this bracelet. With the addition of the house, more of the story is revealed. This isn't a bracelet about birds in trees; it's a story about growing, leaving the nest, and finding beauty in soaring on your own. The two glass beads offer a magical glowing quality that speaks of finding beauty within.

Gardens

Into the garden I step, past iron gates and paths lined with stones. Into the garden I creep, past flowers cultivated and pruned. In the garden, I see life bursting from every corner. In the vibrant hues of flowers and in their graceful shape, there is inspiration. From the industrious bee to dew drops on petals, each detail in the garden offers a world of creative discovery.

Daffodil Fields
Necklace

Anne Choi pendant,
Stephanie Ann Beads disks

supplies

- 25–35 mm focal bead, sterling silver
- 20 mm lampworked disk bead
- **6** 1-in. (2.5 cm) rectangular chain links, sterling silver
- **2** 8 mm flat spacers, sterling silver
- **28** 6 mm faceted citrine disks
- **25** 11º nickel seed beads
- **19** 1-in. headpins, gunmetal
- **2** 2-in. (5 cm) eyepins, gunmetal
- 4 in. 20-gauge sterling silver wire
- **34** 4 mm jump rings, gunmetal
- **12** 2-in. lengths oval link chain, gunmetal
- **4** 1-in. lengths oval link chain, gunmetal
- magnetic flower clasp, gunmetal

finished length: 21 in. (53 cm) with a 2¾ in. (7 cm) dangle

basics

- plain loop
- wrapped loop
- opening and closing jump rings

1

Clustered dangle:

A String a seed bead and a citrine disk on a headpin and make a plain loop above the beads. Make 19 dangles.

Connect three dangles, slip on a jump ring, pick up two dangles, and close the jump ring. Open a jump ring and string the unit just made and two dangles. Close the ring. Open a jump ring and string the unit just made and four dangles. Add two more four-dangle sections in the same way.

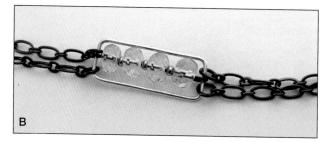

B

Connectors:

B String four citrine disks alternating with seed beads on an eyepin. Make a loop above the beads.

C

Pendant base:

C On the 20-gauge wire, make a wrapped loop at one end. String the focal bead, a spacer, a disk, a spacer, and a citrine bead. Make a wrapped loop above the beads.

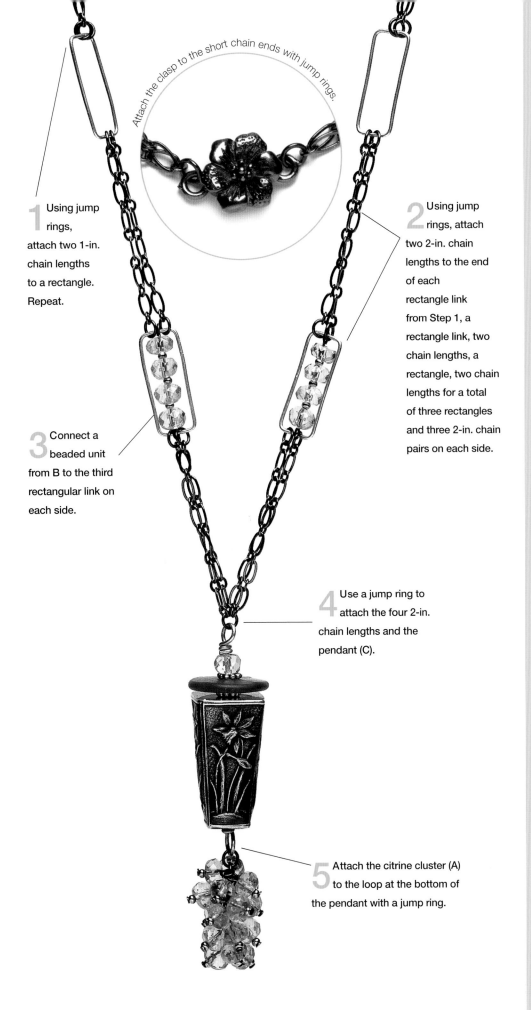

Attach the clasp to the short chain ends with jump rings.

1 Using jump rings, attach two 1-in. chain lengths to a rectangle. Repeat.

2 Using jump rings, attach two 2-in. chain lengths to the end of each rectangle link from Step 1, a rectangle link, two chain lengths, a rectangle, two chain lengths for a total of three rectangles and three 2-in. chain pairs on each side.

3 Connect a beaded unit from B to the third rectangular link on each side.

4 Use a jump ring to attach the four 2-in. chain lengths and the pendant (C).

5 Attach the citrine cluster (A) to the loop at the bottom of the pendant with a jump ring.

Some beads are little works of art and could sit on a shelf to be admired as such. The trouble is, it can be hard to feel like those art beads will be done justice in a jewelry design—there is a fear they will be swallowed up by a supporting cast of beads. I feel that way about Anne Choi's beads—they are so amazing, it's hard to create a design that doesn't distract from their simple and understated beauty. My goal for this design was to create a necklace that let the art bead tell the story. Picking up on the color of the daffodils that one would imagine in this silver rendition, I created a lush pendant of faceted citrine dangles. Each part of this necklace is carefully considered to relate to and accent the art bead. From the silver links in the geometric design to the oval link cable chain and subtle grey of the lampworked disk bead—each part speaks to the art bead without overpowering it.

Titania's Bower Necklace

Elaine Ray ceramic rounds and lentils, seaurchin ceramic flower, Gaea ceramic rounds, Humblebeads polymer clay, Sue Beads lampworked beads, Cindy Gimbrone lampworked headpins

supplies

- 40 mm brass lily pendant
- 30 mm ceramic flower
- 26 mm ceramic lentil
- 25 mm polymer clay lentil
- 20 mm lampworked bead
- 18 mm ceramic lentil
- **4** 12 mm ceramic rounds
- **6** 12 mm lampworked beads
- **2** 10 mm ceramic rounds
- **6** 6 x 9 mm Czech glass flowers
- **12** 6 mm lepidolite rondelles
- **6** 6 mm round glass beads
- **6** 6 mm crystal bicones
- **2** 22 mm brass flower bead caps
- **7** double-dipped lampworked headpins
- **20** copper 11º seed beads
- **6** 4 mm copper flat spacers
- **10** 15 mm jump rings
- **24** 2-in. (5 cm) copper headpins
- **6** 2-in. copper ball headpins
- **2** 2-in. lengths of brass chain
- 28-in. (71 cm) 18-gauge brass wire cut into seven 4-in. (10 cm) lengths

finished length: 18½ in. (47 cm)

basics

- wire tendrils
- wire-wrapped link
- opening and closing jump rings

1 With the ceramic flower in the center, connect the links (A) and (C) with 15 mm jump rings.

2 Use roundnose pliers to make a loop in the center of a double-dipped headpin, then create wire curls with the remaining wire. Make six, and attach one to each jump ring between the beaded links.

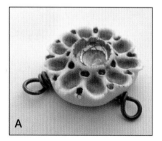

A Make a wire-wrapped link with the ceramic flower, each lentil, and the 20 mm lampworked bead.

B, C Make a wire-wrapped link with three 6 mm glass beads and the flower beadcap. Make two flower links.

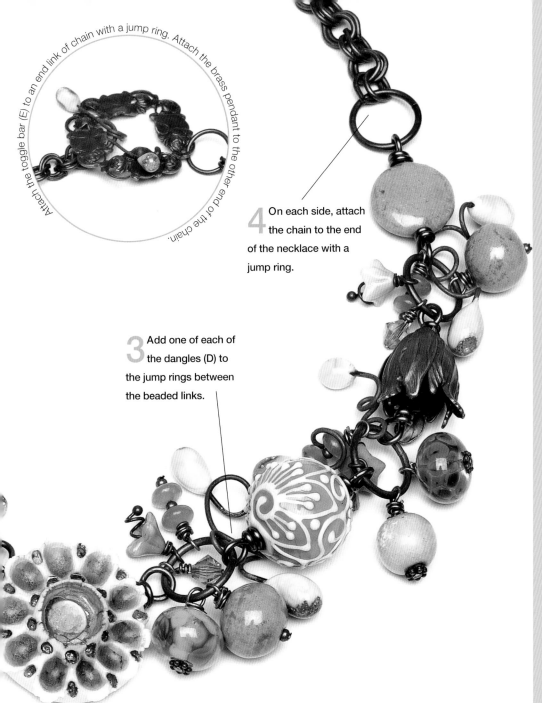

Attach the toggle bar (E) to an end link of chain with a jump ring. Attach the brass pendant to the other end of the chain.

4 On each side, attach the chain to the end of the necklace with a jump ring.

3 Add one of each of the dangles (D) to the jump rings between the beaded links.

The inspiration for this necklace is the fairy queen from Shakespeare's *A Midsummer Night's Dream*. I started this necklace by collecting a pleasing palette of art beads in pastel shades. The accents took their cue from the art beads, playing with colors and texturing in the larger beads. Some components are so rare you have to invent your own use for them, as in the case with Cindy Gimbrone's double-dipped lampworked headpins. I created a fringe by wrapping them several times around my roundnose pliers. The results are whimsical and add a little magic to the design.

D

E

D Make six of each:
- seed bead and ceramic round wrapped dangle
- flat spacer and lampworked bead wrapped dangle
- seed bead, lepidolite, seed bead, and lepidolite wrapped dangle
- bicone crystal wrapped dangle
- flower and a tendril-wrapped balled headpin wrapped dangle

E At the center of a double-dipped headpin, make two loops to form a toggle bar.

The Design Journal

You may feel like only so-called real artists keep sketchbooks, but I say anyone who wants a place to keep their ideas close at hand should create a design journal. A design journal can be your personal space to organize and collect your inspirations. Use your design journal as a resource when researching a new idea or go back through it when you're stumped to spark your imagination. I never have enough time for all the ideas that pop into my head; a sketchbook helps me keep those ideas until I can devote more time to them.

Keep a small sketchbook on hand to doodle and jot down ideas. A pocket-sized Moleskine sketchbook is a nice little treat; the Italian-made paper is silky smooth. A pencil or pen is all you really need to sketch out your ideas. If you'd like to add color, try watercolor pencils with a small brush and water.

"But I can't draw," you say! Don't place a value of good or bad on your sketches—they are simply to help you plan out an idea or capture an inspiration before your fleeting memory tosses that brilliant design into the ether. The good news about drawing beads is that they aren't that complicated to sketch out. A bead can be broken down into its simplest shapes to express an idea. Add little notes to your sketches in case you forget what that blue circle was supposed to be.

You may not be convinced that a sketchbook can help your designs, so you might want to try creating a design idea book. This is a journal where you collect images, ephemera, magazine pictures, or little snips from catalogs and create collages with them. You can cut out images from bead catalogs or magazines and add them to your book. Visit a scrapbook supply store to collect images and mixed-media pieces to add to your journal. Explore whatever inspires you and have fun with your design book. Leave space to jot down ideas. You never know where your next idea will come from.

from the pages of
Heather's sketchbook

A Conversation with Kerri Fuhr

Kerri's lampworked beads of insects, birds, horses, and flowers are paintings created with molten glass. Her beads look like they jumped off the page of a nature-inspired sketchbook. Colors and textures are brushed with flame and glass to create an artistic interpretation of wildlife from her Canadian frontier.

Digital Collages

Another fun source of inspiration is to create digital collages or a color palette based on your photos. Look for online tutorials on how to create a digital collage using design software from the resources below. Pick colors, patterns, shapes, and textures in the collages and then round up beads to reflect your inspiration.

A few handy resources:
Photoshop—a premium photo editing and design software program that is loaded with features.
Gimp—a free photo editing and design software program that can be dowloaded from gimp.org.
Picnik—upload photos from your computer and use the collage generator at picnik.com.
Color Palette Generator—Upload a photo and create a color palette based on the image. Try bighugelabs.com.

Q: What is your process when creating new beads—do you sketch your ideas or work from reference material? When looking for new inspiration, how influential is the natural world around you?

A: I am very inspired by nature and often gain ideas for new beads by what I see outside in the world around me. I spent my childhood living on a mountain in central British Columbia, where I played and explored every day outside in the woods. Deer, eagles, hawks, coyotes, and black bears would often walk near my home, and those encounters have greatly influenced the creative work I do today. Even now, living in the Lower Mainland outside of Vancouver, B.C., I see wildlife often. Last year, two beautiful eagles perched in a tree in my neighbor's yard so I rushed to get my camera and take a few photos of them. I used the photos as a reference to create my eagle portrait beads. I also have an abundance of crows that visit my yard. They are so smart and crafty, and it's always a joy to capture them in glass. When I am inspired to create a new bird, insect, or animal on my beads, I study them in person (if possible) at first and then do extensive research in books and search for photos on the internet so that I can study them in detail. I also often create sketches of ideas but sometimes I just sit at the torch and play. The most delightful surprises can happen that way!

Medieval Medallion Necklace

Gabriel polymer clay bead

supplies

- 48 mm flower filigree square
- 32 mm polymer clay bead
- **3** 12 mm amber chips
- **3** 8 mm faceted glass rondelles
- **11** 6 mm blue labradorite rondelles
- **34** 4 mm copper flat spacers
- 10 mm brass jump ring
- **17** 1-in. (2.5 cm) brass eyepins
- 28 in. (71 cm) brass oval cable chain

finished length including dangle: 37 in. (0.94 m)

basics

- plain loop links
- opening and closing jump rings

Earrings

Glass flowers strung on beaded headpins dangle between pearls and metal leaves, and mimic the detail in the necklace's gorgeous focal bead.

A Create 17 looped links with one flat spacer, one rondelle or chip, and one spacer on an eyepin. Make the loops perpendicular.

B Cut chain into one ¼-in. (6 mm), one ¾-in. (1.9 cm), one 1¼-in. (3.2 cm), one 1¾-in. (4.4 cm), two 2-in. (5 cm), two 2¼ -in. (5.7 cm), and one 11½-in. (29.2 cm) lengths.

Author's Note:
Blue labradorite was a rare bead show find; you can substitute them with iolite, kyanite, or sodalite.

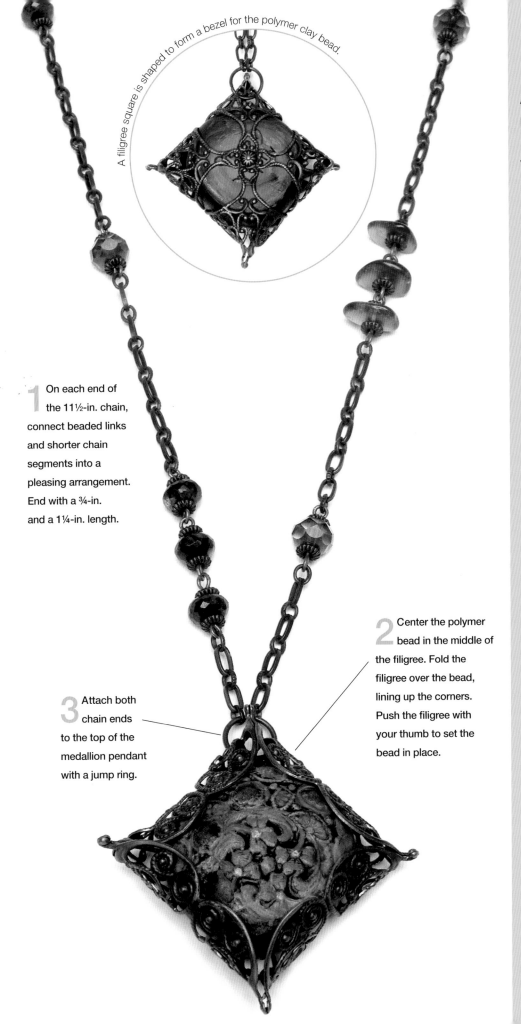

A filigree square is shaped to form a bezel for the polymer clay bead.

A brass filigree pendant captures a Renaissance-inspired floral bead. The chain is divided up by clusters of beads in hues that match the focal and add a touch of color. Using small accents of color in the pendant draws the eye back to the hand-painted bead. The amber beads are a pop of complementary color to break up the monochromatic color palette. A necklace can go from nice to noteworthy if you include complementary colors in small doses.

1 On each end of the 11½-in. chain, connect beaded links and shorter chain segments into a pleasing arrangement. End with a ¾-in. and a 1¼-in. length.

2 Center the polymer bead in the middle of the filigree. Fold the filigree over the bead, lining up the corners. Push the filigree with your thumb to set the bead in place.

3 Attach both chain ends to the top of the medallion pendant with a jump ring.

Flight of the Bumblebee
Bracelet

Kerri Fuhr focal,
Green Girl Studios clasp

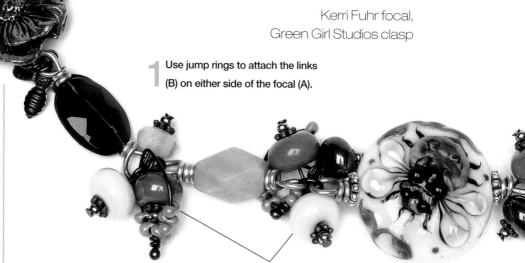

1 Use jump rings to attach the links (B) on either side of the focal (A).

2 At each connection, use jump rings to attach three dangles (C) and one leaf (E).

supplies

- 25 mm lampworked focal
- **2** 15 mm faceted puffed ovals, smoky quartz
- **3** 10 mm faceted barrels, peach aventurine
- **12** 8 mm lampworked spacers
- **3** 7 mm faceted disks, blue lace agate
- **2** 7 mm spacers, sterling silver
- **15** 5 mm spacers, copper
- bee brass charm
- bee and flower pewter hook-and-eye clasp
- **30** 2 x 4 mm tan peanut beads
- **15** 11º nickel seed beads
- **12** 5 mm jump rings, gunmetal
- **5** 2-in. (5 cm) ball headpins, gunmetal
- **15** 1-in. (2.5 cm) headpins, gunmetal
- 4-in. (10 cm) length sterling silver 20-gauge wire
- 15 in. (38 cm) sterling silver 20-gauge wire, cut into five 3-in. (7.6 cm) lengths

finished length:
  7½ in. (19.1 cm)

basics

- wire-wrapped links
- opening and closing jump rings

A Wire-wrap the focal bead with silver spacers on either side.

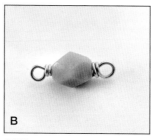

B Wire-wrap five stone links with the aventurine and smoky quartz beads.

C Create dangles: String a nickel seed bead, a copper spacer, and a lampworked spacer or blue lace agate bead on a headpin. Make a loop above the beads. Make 15 dangles.

Back of focal bead.

Earrings

Make a pair of matching earrings by alternating three flat spacers and two lampworked spacers on an eyepin. Make a loop above the beads. Attach a wire leaf and bee charm to the bottom of the eyepin with a small jump ring. Attach an earring wire to the top of the eyepin. Make a second earring.

3 Use jump rings to attach a clasp half to each end. Attach a bee charm to the flower side of the clasp.

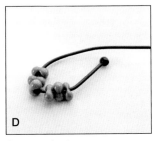

D   E

Create wire leaves:
D Bend a balled headpin in half to form a V and string six peanut seed beads.
E Wrap the wire end around the ball end of the headpin two times. Shape the wire with chainnose pliers to define the leaf. Make five leaves.

This design is all about the details. To enhance the delicate and lyrical focal bead, I created elements inspired by the color and line of the bee. I was lucky enough to pick up spacers by the same bead artist and let those colors guide my choices. The wings instantly reminded me of blue lace agate, and the peach aventurine and smoky quartz colors can be seen in the bee's body. I created "flower" clusters between each stone link, as if the bee was hovering above a garden.

Taking this design from a simple dangle bracelet, I added an unexpected twist—wire-wrapped leaves accented by seed beads. They were created using ball headpins and work great with the black lines on the focal bead. Finally, the perfect clasp for this bracelet—a hook-and-eye bee and flower!

Zen Garden Bracelet

Humblebeads polymer clay beads,
Blue Seraphim lampworked bead

supplies

- **4** 20 mm polymer clay 2-hole spacers
- 20 mm stick pearl
- **2** 12 mm coin pearls
- 14 mm lampworked disk
- 10 mm smoky quartz bead
- **4** 8–10 mm pearls
- **3** 8 mm double-drilled pearls
- 8 mm faceted glass rondelle
- **5** keishi pearls
- **7** 6 mm round beads (stones or pearls)
- **2** 6 mm faceted glass rondelles
- **6** 6 mm bicone crystals
- **2** silver 4 mm flat flower spacers
- **2** silver 4 mm flat flower spacers
- **2** g 11º nickel seed beads (color A)
- **5** g 11º brown iris seed beads (color B)
- **2** g Delicas (color C)
- 35 mm toggle bar
- Fireline 6 lb. test
- beading needle

finished length: 8 in. (20 cm)

FIGURE 1

FIGURE 2

Bracelet base

1 Cut 3 ft. (0.9 m) of Fireline and thread a needle on it. Pick up a color A 11º seed bead and sew through it again for a stopper bead. Pick up 30 As and sew back through the stopper bead **(figure 1, a–b)**.

2 Pick up a 6 mm crystal, a 4 mm spacer, a 10 mm round, an A, and a double-drilled pearl (b–c).

3 For row 1 of the base, pick up 14 color B 11º seed beads and one side of a 2-hole polymer clay spacer bead (c–d). Repeat three times.

4 Pick up 14 more Bs, a double-drilled pearl, an A, a 6 mm rondelle, a 3 mm spacer, a 6 mm crystal, six As, and the toggle bar. Skip the six As, and sew back through the previous five beads **(figure 2, a–b)**.

5 Working as in step 3, pick up 14 Bs, and sew through the other hole of the next polymer clay spacer (b–c). Repeat along the base to add a second span of Bs between each pair of spacers. After picking up the last set of 14 Bs, sew through the beads you picked up in step 2.

6 Working counter clockwise, sew through the first two As **(figure 3, a–b)**. Work a round of

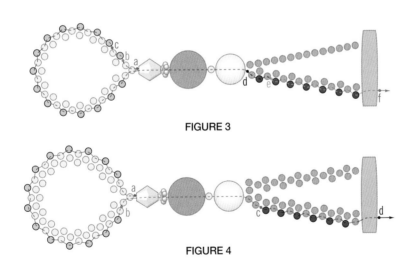

FIGURE 3

FIGURE 4

peyote stitch around the loop: Pick up an A, skip the next A in the loop, and sew through the following A (b–c). Repeat around the loop, then sew back through the first A and the next five beads (c–d).

7 For row 2 of the base, sew through the first B. Working in peyote, pick up a B, skip the next B in row 1, and sew through the following B (d–e). Repeat across the segment of Bs, and sew through the next polymer spacer (e–f). Repeat this step across the row, sewing through the five ends beads after you've worked peyote stitch across all the B segments.

8 Sew through the loop of As attaching the toggle bar, and continue through the next five beads. Repeat step 7 to work peyote stitch along the other B segments, then sew through the five large beads at the other end.

9 Sew through the first three As, then work in peyote around the clasp loop **(figure 4, a–b)**. Sew through the next two As, five large beads, and the first two Bs in the following segment of Bs (b–c).

10 Working as in step 7, stitch a row of peyote across all the segments of Bs. After you've stitched across the end segment, pick up four

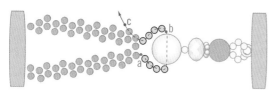

FIGURE 5

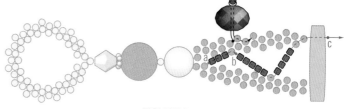

FIGURE 6

As, and sew through the side hole of the double-drilled pearl **(figure 5, a–b)**. Pick up four As, and sew through the end B on the other side (b–c). Work peyote to the other end.

11 To complete the base, you need to add stitches bridging the gap between the peyote segments. There is not a specific thread path, but the general direction is as follows: Sew through the beadwork to exit the first B on the inner edge of a peyote segment. Pick up three color C cylinder beads, cross over the gap between the peyote segments, and sew through the nearest inner B on the other segment **(figure 6, a–b)**. Repeat this process, adding three to seven Cs per stitch and sewing through the next polymer spacer when you get to it (b–c). Work in this manner to bridge all the sets of peyote segments.

Fringe embellishment

Arrange your embellishment beads in a balanced pattern of four to six beads per segment. The larger beads should go in the center of the bracelet.

1 Sew through three to four seed beads in the base. Pick up an embellishment bead and an A. Sew back through the embellishment bead and the closest bead in the base. Keep the tension pulled tight to attach the embellishments securely.

2 Sew through three beads and add another embellishment bead.

3 Sew through a few Bs to get to the first bridge of Delicas and sew through to get to the other side of the bracelet. Sew through two or three base beads and add another embellishment bead. Repeat to add one to three more embellishment beads. Cross back through the next bridge and add one or two embellishment beads on the other side. Sew through the following polymer clay spacer and repeat until you reach the end of the bracelet.

4 When you reach the double-drilled pearl: Pick up four As and sew through the hole side of the double-drilled pearl. Pick up four As and sew back through first B bead. Continue adding embellishment beads as desired.

5 Sew back through the beads and tie a knot. Repeat several times, and trim the Fireline.

To add more Fireline: when you have 6 in. (15 cm) of Fireline left, cut another 3 ft. Tie the new thread to the base of the short tail on the backside of the beadwork. Tie another knot to secure, weave all of the loose threads into the beadwork, and trim.

Size: To adjust the size of your bracelet, increase or decrease the number of Bs in each segment of Bs in row 1.
12 = 6¾ in. (17.1 cm)
14 = 7⅜ in. (18.7 cm)
16 = 8-in. (20 cm)

Variation

By changing the color palette to teals, cream, and white, this bracelet can look like an underwater garden.

Garden Gate Earrings

Lynn Davis polymer clay beads

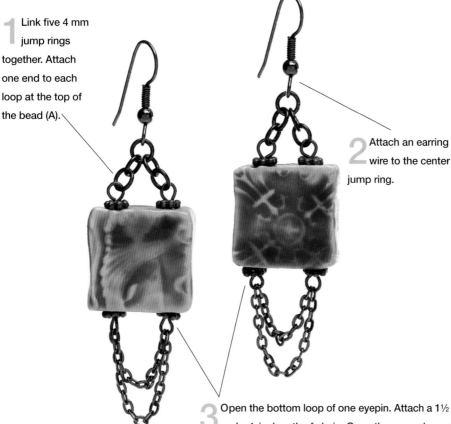

1 Link five 4 mm jump rings together. Attach one end to each loop at the top of the bead (A).

2 Attach an earring wire to the center jump ring.

3 Open the bottom loop of one eyepin. Attach a 1½ in. and a 1-in. length of chain. Open the second eyepin and attach the end links of the chains. Close the loops. Make a second earring.

supplies

- 20 mm double-holed polymer clay beads
- **10** 4 mm gunmetal jump rings
- **8** 4 mm antiqued copper flat spacers
- **4** 1½-in. (3.8 cm) gunmetal eyepins
- **2** gunmetal earring wires
- 5 in. gunmetal chain cut into two 1½-in and two 1-in. (2.5 cm) lengths

basics

- plain loop
- opening and closing a jump ring

A On an eyepin, string a spacer, one hole of the bead, and a spacer. Make a loop above the beads. Repeat for the remaining hole.

Taking my cue from the architectural element of the polymer clay beads, I kept this design minimal with gunmetal chain and rings. The double-holed beads offer the framework for draping chain; the dramatic effect resembles the old wrought-iron gates found in lush Southern gardens.

Thistles & Blooms
Necklace

Chinook Jewelry pendant and connector,
Holly Gage clasp and bead cap

supplies

- 37 mm ceramic pendant
- **8** 20 mm wooden beads
- **14** 20 mm pink biwa stick pearls
- **2** 10 mm pink lampworked disks
- **4** 8 mm smoky quartz beads
- **9** 8 mm muscovite rondelles
- **6** 8 mm dark red pearls
- **8** 6 mm raspberry pearls
- **22** 6 mm rhodonite rondelles
- **10** 6 mm lepidolite rondelles
- 2 g pink 8º seed beads
- 2 g copper 11º seed beads
- 2 g nickel 11º seed beads
- 2 g bronze bugle beads
- 18 mm ceramic connector
- 19 mm x 12 mm silver flower bead cap
- 18 mm x 27 mm silver leaf S-clasp
- **8** 8 mm silver jump rings
- **2** 2 mm silver crimp tubes
- 2-in sterling silver 22-gauge wire
- 3 20-in. lengths of flexible beading wire

finished length:
18 in. (46 cm)

basics

- crimping
- wrapped loop
- opening and closing a jump ring
- attaching a clasp

Author's Note:

Use a bead stopper or tape to hold your beads in place while stringing this multi-strand necklace.

Bracelet

Use a pewter button from Mamacita Beadworks in a chrysanthemum pattern with a row of stick pearls to create a matching bracelet. On 10 in. (25 cm) of beading wire, string 7–8 in. (18–20 cm) of pearls with nickel seed beads between each. String a crimp tube and a pewter button, and thread the wire back through the crimp. Crimp the crimp tube. On the other side, string a crimp tube and 27 nickel seed beads. Thread the beading wire back though the crimp tube to form a loop, crimp the crimp tube, and trim the wire.

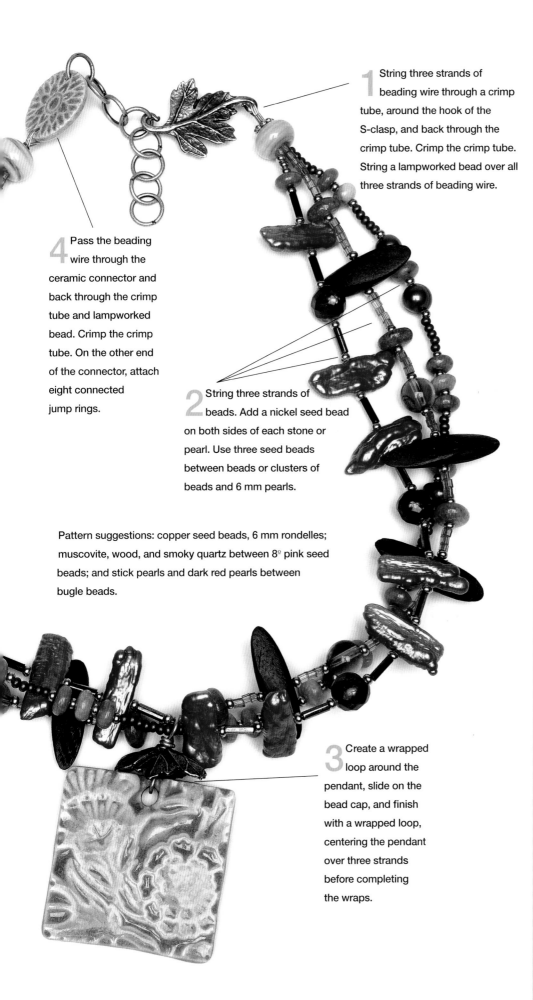

1 String three strands of beading wire through a crimp tube, around the hook of the S-clasp, and back through the crimp tube. Crimp the crimp tube. String a lampworked bead over all three strands of beading wire.

4 Pass the beading wire through the ceramic connector and back through the crimp tube and lampworked bead. Crimp the crimp tube. On the other end of the connector, attach eight connected jump rings.

2 String three strands of beads. Add a nickel seed bead on both sides of each stone or pearl. Use three seed beads between beads or clusters of beads and 6 mm pearls.

Pattern suggestions: copper seed beads, 6 mm rondelles; muscovite, wood, and smoky quartz between 8º pink seed beads; and stick pearls and dark red pearls between bugle beads.

3 Create a wrapped loop around the pendant, slide on the bead cap, and finish with a wrapped loop, centering the pendant over three strands before completing the wraps.

A floral bead cap adds a unique flair to a plain wrapped-loop bail for this ceramic pendant. A luscious collection of three strands of pearls, wood, and stones are interspersed among metallic seed beads in copper and nickel. With three strands of beading wire, it's a good idea to end the strands with a larger-hole bead like the lampworked spacers used here. The back of the necklace has some hidden elements with a leaf-shaped S-clasp, a ceramic connector mirroring the pendant, and a necklace extender created from jump rings.

Dragonfly Pond Necklace

Sea of Glass lampworked rings,
Humblebeads Polymer clay

supplies

- 50 x 39 mm brass ornate dragonfly
- 47 x 35 mm brass Art Deco dragonfly
- 30 mm polymer clay lentil bead
- **2** 35 mm lampworked rings
- 25 mm lampworked ring
- **3** 25 mm melon resin coins
- 14 mm polymer clay disk
- **3** 6 mm olivine resin beads
- **2** 4 mm copper flat spacers
- **5** 15 mm brass jump rings
- 10 mm brass etched jump rings
- **5** 4 mm brass jump rings
- **6** 1 in. brass eyepins
- 2 in. brass eyepin
- brass lobster claw clasp
- 18 in. (46 cm) brass oval link chain, cut into four 4½-in. (11.4 cm) lengths

finished length: 22 in. (56 cm)

basics

- plain loop
- loop links
- opening and closing jump rings

Earrings

These earrings remind me of drops of rain cascading down a decorative downspout. Make them by alternating 6 mm Czech crystals with beadcaps and adding a tiny dragonfly charm at the end.

Dragonfly wrapped bead:
A Wrap the wings and tail of a dragonfly around the lentil bead using flatnose pliers.
B String the lentil bead on a 2-in. eyepin and make a loop on the other end.

Dragonfly link:
C Use roundnose pliers to create a loop with the filigree dragonfly tail.

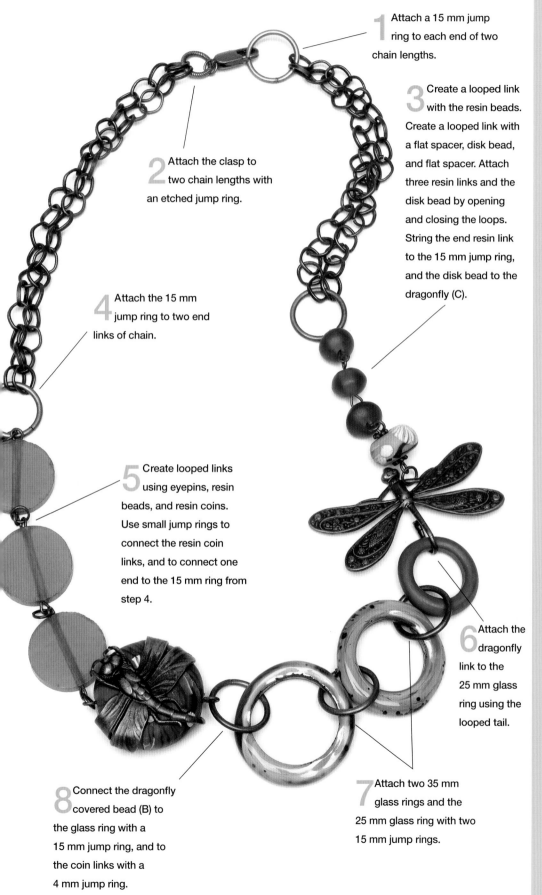

1 Attach a 15 mm jump ring to each end of two chain lengths.

2 Attach the clasp to two chain lengths with an etched jump ring.

3 Create a looped link with the resin beads. Create a looped link with a flat spacer, disk bead, and flat spacer. Attach three resin links and the disk bead by opening and closing the loops. String the end resin link to the 15 mm jump ring, and the disk bead to the dragonfly (C).

4 Attach the 15 mm jump ring to two end links of chain.

5 Create looped links using eyepins, resin beads, and resin coins. Use small jump rings to connect the resin coin links, and to connect one end to the 15 mm ring from step 4.

6 Attach the dragonfly link to the 25 mm glass ring using the looped tail.

7 Attach two 35 mm glass rings and the 25 mm glass ring with two 15 mm jump rings.

8 Connect the dragonfly covered bead (B) to the glass ring with a 15 mm jump ring, and to the coin links with a 4 mm jump ring.

Glass ring "lily pads" host a pair of dragonflies as they buzz among leaves and flowers. The rule of three comes into play here with three rings, disks, and coins. Resin offers a glow of color without adding weight to the design. The dark antiqued brass plays off the warm colors in this necklace, reminding me of sunlight dappling through trees on a languid summer day.

Forget Me Knot Necklace

Lisa Peters raku ceramic pendant

supplies

- 40 mm ceramic flower pendant
- 32 mm brass filigree drop
- 8 mm rhinestone bead
- **2** 7 mm brass bead cones
- **2** 6 mm bicone crystals
- **3** 2-in. (5 cm) brass ball headpins
- **9** 4 mm brass jump rings
- 37¾ in. (0.96 m) 2 mm brass cable chain cut into ½- (1.3 cm), ¾- (1.9 cm), 1½- (3.8 cm), 2- (5 cm), and 33-in. (84 cm) lengths

basics

- opening and closing jump rings
- plain loop
- wrapped bail (earrings)
- crimping (earrings)

A

B

C

Dangles:

A String a crystal and cone on a headpin and make a loop above the cone. Make two. With jump rings, attach one dangle to a ¾-in. chain length and one to a 2-in. chain length.

B String a rhinestone bead on a headpin and make a loop above the bead. Attach to a 1½-in. chain length with a jump ring.

C Use a jump ring to attach the filigree teardrop to a 1½-in. chain length.

D

E

Creating the chain beads:

D Tie a double knot in the long chain 7-in. (18 cm) from the end.

E Use a jump ring to attach two knots together on the front. (The back of the knot is flat.) Close the jump ring. Repeat to make another knot 2 in. away. Create two more knots on the other side of chain, spacing the knots out.

1 Attach the ends of the long knotted chain to the pendant with a jump ring.

2 Attach the four chain dangles to the bottom of the ceramic pendant with a jump ring.

Earrings

A matching pair of earrings with porcelain disk beads from Earthenwood studios uses ball headpins to create wire bails for the disks.

supplies

- **2** 15 mm ceramic disks
- **2** 10 mm lampworked spacers
- **2** 8 mm amazonite faceted rondelles
- **2** 8 mm brass flower bead caps
- **2** 6 mm faceted round crystal beads
- **2** 2-in. antique copper ball headpins
- **2** 2-in. brass kidney ear wires
- **2** 2 mm brass crimp tubes

1 Create a wrapped bail with the headpin for the ceramic disk bead.

2 On the kidney wire, string the round crystal, beadcap, lampworked bead, amazonite, and crimp tube. Use crimping pliers to crimp the crimp tube to the earring wires.

The accent "beads" in this necklace are really knotted chain. The delicate chain is host to a texturally exciting ceramic raku pendant. A quartet of dangles plays with color and shapes in a romantic collection of brass, crystals, and rhinestones.

he held
her like a
seashell
& listened
to her
(heart)

Sea

Being near water brings peace to my spirit. From waves lapping on the shore to the feel of sand beneath my toes, when I'm at the ocean I am home. Cool Caribbean waters surrounding tropical islands infuse their bright, clear turquoise into my soul. Tide pools capture my imagination. Beaches filled with rocks and shells are the real buried treasures. The mystery of the deep, where life is seldom seen but often studied, brings colors and designs that are otherworldly. Sea urchins, starfish, and coral wait beneath the surface, holding a world of inspiration for intrepid adventurers.

Effervescence Necklace

Mamacita Beadwork pewter pendant,
Kelley's Beads lampworked headpins

supplies

Necklace:

- 46 mm pewter pendant
- **6** lampworked headpins
- **8** 15 mm jump rings
- 18 mm toggle clasp
- **2** 5 mm jump rings, optional
- 8½-in. (21.6 cm) chain cut into two 4¼-in. (10.8 cm) lengths
- A seed bead tube or a 1¼-in. (3.2 cm) dowel to use as a mandrel

finished length:
  17½ in. (44.5 cm)

Earrings:

- **2** 30 mm pewter connectors
- **2** 16 mm lampworked disks
- **2** 15 mm brass jump rings
- **2** 4 mm gunmetal jump rings
- 3¼ in. (7.6 cm) 2 mm copper cable chain cut into four ¾-in. (1.9 cm) lengths
- **2** links from necklace chain
- pair of brass earring wires

basics

- opening and closing a jump ring

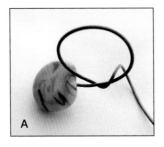

A, B Make a ring from a headpin by forming the headpin wire around the bead tube/ dowel and wrapping the tail to secure the loop. Repeat with all the headpins.

C Open an end link of chain to attach a clasp.

Earrings

Pair lampworked beads by Blue Seraphim with pewter connectors and copper chain.

1 Open a 15 mm jump ring and string the connector, a disk bead, and link of copper chain. Close the jump ring.
2 Open a 4 mm jump ring and attach two lengths of 2 mm chain to the bottom of the connector. Close the jump ring.
3 Connect the earring wires to the copper link.
4 Make a second earring.

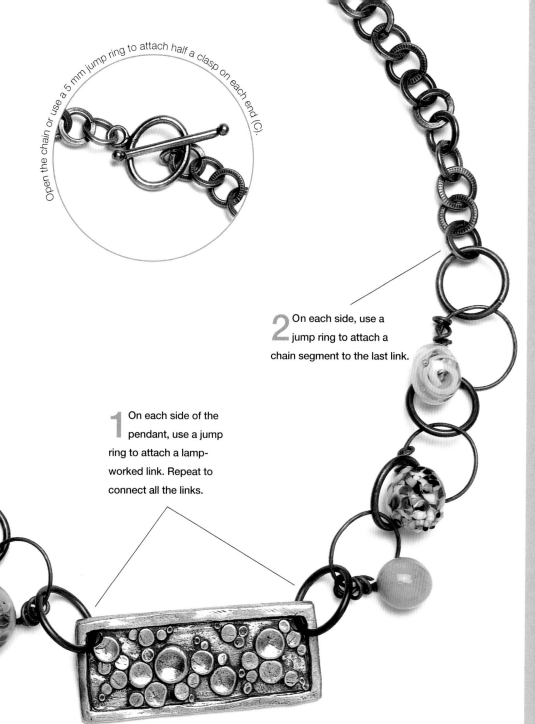

Open the chain or use a 5 mm jump ring to attach half a clasp on each end (C).

2 On each side, use a jump ring to attach a chain segment to the last link.

1 On each side of the pendant, use a jump ring to attach a lamp-worked link. Repeat to connect all the links.

Feeling bubbly? When I was playing with these lampworked headpins, I kept thinking I wanted to show them off in some type of sculptural design. I decided to create a chain transforming the head-pins into wire-wrapped links. Everything about this necklace relates to the light and airy circle motif. From rings made of glass headpins, to the circle chain, to the clasp, each part ties back to the bubble design of the pewter pendant. Mixing metals adds a modern touch to this design that seamlessly blends pewter, brass, and copper.

Into the Deep Necklace

Pam Wynn polymer clay beads, Diane Hawkey faceted ceramic beads, Elaine Ray round ceramic bead, Green Girl Studios shibuichi clasp, Starlia Phillips lampworked ruffles

supplies

- 35 mm glass seashell
- 22 mm glass seashell
- **4** 22 mm lampworked ruffle disks
- **2** 20 mm glass rugged coins
- **5** 18 mm polymer clay coins
- 15 mm ceramic faceted bead
- **2** 14 mm x 10 mm smoky quartz faceted ovals
- **13** 12 mm buri nut beads
- 12 mm ceramic faceted bead
- 12 mm ceramic round bead
- 12 mm x 8 mm smoky quartz tab
- 10 mm aventurine faceted rondelle
- **2** 8 mm rhinestone beads
- 6 mm smoky quartz round bead
- 30 mm shibuichi seashell clasp
- **2** 12 mm silver flat spacers
- 10 mm silver flat spacers
- **4** 8 mm silver flat spacers
- **4** 6 mm silver flat spacers
- **8** 4 mm silver flat spacers
- **6** 10 mm brass etched jump rings
- **2** 2 mm silver crimp tubes
- 25 in. (64 cm) flexible beading wire

finished length:
   19¾ in. (50.2 cm)

basics

- attaching a clasp
- crimping
- opening and closing a jump ring

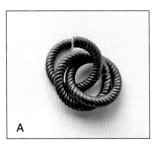 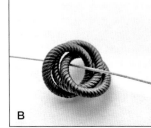

A, B Make a knotted rosette spacer by linking two jump rings and then linking a third through both. Make two.

2 String a smoky quartz oval, 13 buri beads, and a smoky quartz oval.

3 String a 4 mm spacer, a rugged coin, a 6 mm spacer, a 12 mm faceted ceramic bead, a 6 mm spacer, a ceramic round bead, a polymer clay coin, a 4 mm spacer, a rhinestone bead, a 22 mm shell, a 4 mm flat spacer, a polymer clay coin, a 4 mm flat spacer, and a polymer clay coin.

The deep and dark briny sea is the inspiration for this strung necklace. A necklace that is simple in technique can be visually complex. From a mix of textural components from bumpy polymer clay, ruffled glass, and rustic ceramic to an interesting metal clasp shaped like a nautilus, each part of this necklace is an underwater inspired jewel. The focal points of the necklace are three shells: two realistic lampworked glass beads, and one created from a series of disks and decreasing metal spacers to mimic the shape of the shell bead. A trio of jump rings form rope-like spacers; they are the perfect extra detail for this seafaring creation.

1 Crimp one half of the clasp to the beading wire.

6 String a 35 mm glass shell, a smoky quartz round, a rhinestone bead, a polymer clay coin, a 4 mm spacer, a polymer clay coin, a 6 mm spacer, a 15 mm faceted ceramic bead, a jump ring rosette, a rugged coin, a 4 mm spacer, an aventurine rondelle, a 4 mm spacer, and a smoky quartz tab. Crimp the remaining clasp half to the beading wire.

5 String two 12 mm flat spacers, a 10 mm spacer, an 8 mm spacer, and a 6 mm spacer.

4 String a jump ring rosette (B). String a ruffle and an 8 mm spacer. Repeat twice. String a ruffle.

Bronze Nautilus Earrings

Miss Fickle Media polymer clay

Faux bronze fossil beads, pearls, and brass wire create a funky and modern backdrop for these mermaid-approved earrings. The polymer clay beads add volume but not weight to the designs, despite their larger size.

supplies

- **2** 25 mm polymer clay nautilus beads
- **10** 8 mm bronze keishi pearls
- **2** 15 mm brass jump rings
- **2** brass earring wires
- 30 in. (76 cm) brass 24-gauge wire cut into two 15-in. (38 cm) lengths

basics

- opening and closing a jump ring

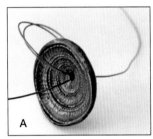
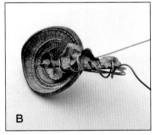

A Thread wire through the center of the polymer clay bead. Wrap the wire twice through the bead, creating two large wire loops. One end of the wire will be in the front of the bead and one behind.

B String a pearl on the front wire, position it snug to the polymer bead, and thread the wire over the top, back through the center hole, and up behind the pearl. String a pearl on the working wire. Wrap loosely around the wire loops and add another pearl. Repeat three times.

C Wrap the wire around the loops until you've used the length. Trim with wire cutters and use chainnose pliers to tighten the wire to the loop.

D Wrap the wire that is behind the bead a few times up the wire loop, trim and tighten the end to the wire loop.

Open a jump ring and connect an earring wire and the wired component. Close the jump ring.

Make a second earring.

Caribbean Waters Bracelet

Cindy Gimbrone lampworked glass rings,
Sue Beads lampworked glass bead

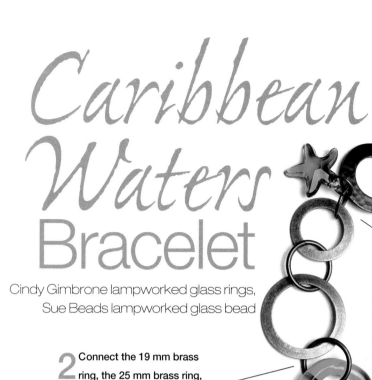

1 Attach the starfish to a 6 mm jump ring. Open a 10 mm jump ring and connect the starfish dangle, the hammered link, and the 19 mm brass ring.

2 Connect the 19 mm brass ring, the 25 mm brass ring, the 20 mm glass ring, and the 30 mm glass ring with 15 mm jump rings.

supplies
- 30 mm lampworked ring
- 25 mm lampworked ring
- 14 mm lampworked disk
- 16 mm crystal starfish
- **2** 22 mm brass filigree rings
- **10** blue 8° seed beads
- 2-in. (5 cm) brass headpin
- 25 mm brass ring
- 19 mm brass ring
- 22 mm brass hammered ring with 1 mm hole
- 24 mm brass pod toggle bar
- **6** 15 mm brass jump rings
- **2** 10 mm brass jump rings
- 6 mm brass jump ring

finished length:
8⅛ in. (20.5 cm)

basics
- opening and closing a jump ring
- plain loop link

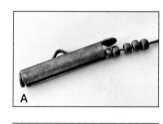

A

B

A, B String 10 seed beads onto the headpin. Place the beaded headpin into the toggle pod. Trim the extra wire and close the pod.

C

C Make a bead link with the glass bead and a headpin. Attach it to the toggle bar with a 10 mm jump ring.

3 Connect the 30 mm glass ring and the two filigree rings with 15 mm jump rings. Attach to the bead link (C) with a 15 mm jump ring.

If you've ever visited a Caribbean island, you'll instantly recognize this blue. It's amazing that the ocean can be this color, and it offers inspiration to artists and designers in every field. I paired these two lampworked glass rings with a series of brass rings for instant nautical appeal. A crystal starfish and lampworked bead bring in some variation to keep the design interesting.

Note:
Adjust the fit by adding a few jump rings before the toggle or by omitting the 19 mm brass ring.

Jellyfish Necklace

Stephanie Ann glass beads

supplies

- 25 mm blown glass bead
- **3** 20 mm lampworked disks
- **33** 6 mm faceted fluorite disks
- **13** 6 mm copper saucer beads
- 23 mm brass starfish charm
- 5-in. (13 cm) 18-gauge brass balled headpin
- **8** 4 mm brass jump rings
- 15 mm brass jump rings
- 18-in. (46 cm) 5 mm brass oval chain cut into four ¾-in. (1.9 cm), two 6-in. (15 cm), and one 3-in. (7.6 cm) lengths
- 33 in. 2 mm brass cable chain cut into four 1-in. (2.5 cm), two 6-in., one 3-in., and one 14-in. (36 cm) lengths
- 12-in. (30 cm) 24-gauge brass wire cut into six 2-in. (5 cm) lengths

finished length: 25 in. (64 cm) plus 5-in. (13 cm) dangle

basics

- opening and closing a jump ring
- wire-wrapped link

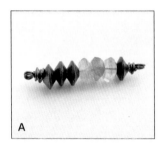

A Make six double wire-wrapped links using brass wire strung with a random pattern of fluorite and copper spacers.

B Attach a 14-in. cable chain length to a fluorite link on each end by opening the chain link or using a jump ring. On each side, use jump rings to connect a fluorite link to two lengths of 1-in. cable chain, a fluorite link, a ¾-in. oval chain, and a fluorite link.

Earrings

Make a wire-wrapped link with a fluorite bead and two brass spacers. Connect three chain segments to the bottom with a jump ring; attach an earring wire to the top.

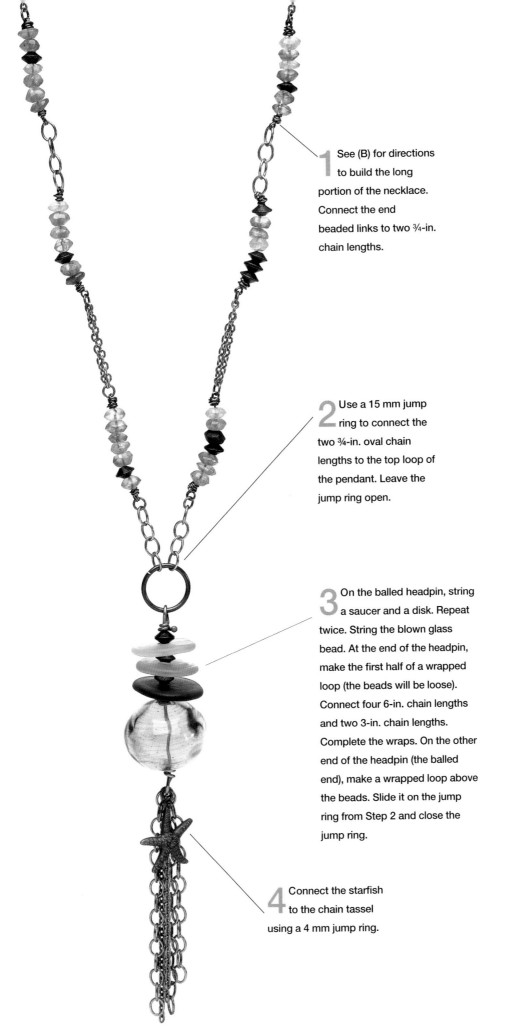

1 See (B) for directions to build the long portion of the necklace. Connect the end beaded links to two ¾-in. chain lengths.

2 Use a 15 mm jump ring to connect the two ¾-in. oval chain lengths to the top loop of the pendant. Leave the jump ring open.

3 On the balled headpin, string a saucer and a disk. Repeat twice. String the blown glass bead. At the end of the headpin, make the first half of a wrapped loop (the beads will be loose). Connect four 6-in. chain lengths and two 3-in. chain lengths. Complete the wraps. On the other end of the headpin (the balled end), make a wrapped loop above the beads. Slide it on the jump ring from Step 2 and close the jump ring.

4 Connect the starfish to the chain tassel using a 4 mm jump ring.

When I saw this blown glass bead, I knew immediately that it would become something inspired by the sea. I paired it with chain lengths and lampworked disks to create a jellyfish. The repetition of the stacked rondelles plays off the stacked disk beads. The chain gives the design a light and airy feeling that complements the hollow bead. I doubled the finer chain to visually balance the larger oval chain. The fluorite beads and disks were a perfect match. Their color and texture are like faux beach glass.

Tide Pool Treasures
Bracelet

Stephanie Ann lampworked bead,
Lynn Davis pewter shell

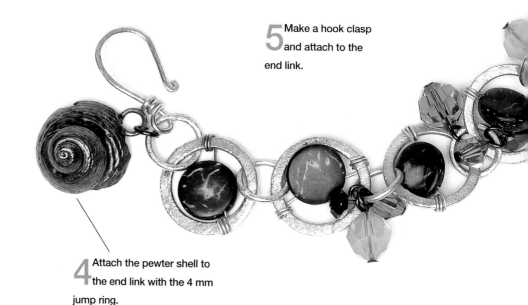

5 Make a hook clasp and attach to the end link.

4 Attach the pewter shell to the end link with the 4 mm jump ring.

supplies

- 28 mm lampworked glass bead
- 20 mm pewter shell
- **8** 10 mm coconut coins
- **6** 8 mm round crystals
- **6** 6 mm crystal bicones
- **6** 6 mm glass rondelles
- 4 mm gunmetal jump ring
- **18** 1-in. (2.5 cm) gunmetal headpins
- 7 in. (18 cm) 16 mm silver long-and-short chain cut into two 3½-in. (8.9 cm) lengths
- 3½ in. 18-gauge sterling silver wire
- 20 in. (51 cm) 24-gauge sterling silver wire cut into eight 2½-in. (6.4 cm) lengths
- 3 in. (7.6 cm) 20-gauge wire

basics

- hook clasp
- plain loop
- opening and closing jump rings
- wire-wrapped link

A

A Make 18 beaded dangles using the round crystals, crystal bicones, and rondelles on headpins.

Bead-onomics

Beads like the intricate lampworked bead shown in this project are time-intensive creations and that labor is reflected in the price, so they may be out of the budget for new beaders or those on a limited income. Don't be afraid to substitute a simpler style of bead that is more within your price range. The variation bead in this project cost about a quarter of the price of the collectable lampworked masterpiece but still offers beach-inspired charm.

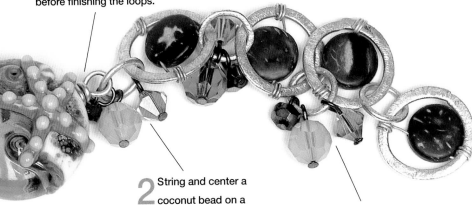

1 Create a wrapped link with the lampworked bead, adding a chain segment on each end before finishing the loops.

2 String and center a coconut bead on a 2½-in. length of wire. Place inside a large chain link and wrap the wire around the link 2–3 times to secure. Repeat on the other side and trim the wire ends. Repeat to wire coconut beads to all eight large links.

3 Attach three dangles (A) to each of the connecting links (a round crystal, a crystal bicone, and a rondelle dangle).

Wire-wrapping tiny coconut beads into the center of the chain links adds visual interest to a simple design. The intricate lampworked bead is paired with accents in matching colors. A rustic pewter seashell provides contrast to the polished glass and complements the brushed metal of the chain.

Variation

This variation uses brass chain and wire with turquoise-colored bicone crystals. A brass starfish pairs with a tide pool-inspired lampworked bead from Blue Seraphim.

Color in Nature

Translating the incredible color inspiration offered by nature into beads can be tricky. First, go on a color hunt. After you find your inspiration source, break down the colors to find the ones you'd like to work with. Finally, match those colors to your beads at the beginning of your design process.

Take photographs of scenes or objects in nature that you find intriguing, or find photos in books, magazines, or online. If you take your own photographs, try to go out in the early morning or right before sunset for the best light. Zoom in on a subject with your macro lens to capture the world within nature's minute details. Or scan the horizon for landscapes that offer a vista of color. Look for places where there is a high contrast of lights and darks or a saturation of colors, like a grove of trees at sunset or a garden bursting with summer blooms. Make a habit of going on color-palette hunts and taking your camera with you to your favorite places.

Either print your photographs or work digitally. Use an online color-palette generator to pick colors for you. This is a quick and easy way to break down colors, and help you unlock the mystery of why you were drawn to a photo. To pick your own colors from a photo, select two or three of the main colors. If you are having a hard time, squint your eyes to see past the images and focus only on the colors. Once you have your main colors, study the photo and pick out a light and dark color for contrast. To help organize your thoughts and to keep a visual record of your color palette, pick these colors out using digital imaging software or match your picks to paint chips. Glue your palette into a design journal or create a color collage with the paint chips.

Nature doesn't have a color wheel, yet you'll never find more harmonious color combinations.

Now that you have inspiration colors, head to your bead boxes and find beads that are a close match to your color palette. You may go with only two of the colors for a design or you might have one dominant color with two or three accent colors. Or you may match up all the colors in your palette. Don't forget to use the color of your metal beads and findings as part of your palette, too.

A Natural Color Wheel

Complementary colors—colors that are directly across the color wheel. Red/green, blue/orange, and purple/yellow are examples. Study these colors in nature to see how they are paired together. Fruits, flowers, and vegetation offer a quick reference for beautiful complementary color combinations.

Analogous colors—colors that are next to each other on the color wheel. Think of the oranges, pinks, and purples of a sunset.

Monochromatic colors—variations of the same color, in tints (white added), shades (gray added), or tones (light and darkness of a color). Monochromatic color schemes work best when there is a variation in the value or tone of the color.

A Conversation with D'Arsie Manzella— Mamacita Beadworks

D'Arsie primarily creates pewter beads; hand-sculpting, casting, grinding, and polishing each and every one. She does occasionally venture into other media, all showcasing themes inspired by nature. I'm drawn to the wonderful textures of her work, the minute details that show the telltale signs of the artist's hand. When I sit down with D'Arsie's beads, it's easy to enter into that mother-earth nature groove that her work exudes.

Q: Texture is everything in your work, whether it's the ebb and flow of seaweed or the impression of feather or flower. How do you find your next inspiration?

A. Inspiration swirls around me daily. I might see a pattern and it will trigger a design. I sometimes dream ideas for my work. Nature inspires me constantly. It is the origin of beauty and cannot go unnoticed. The images and textures I take in are like visual ingredients in a creative melting pot. When I sit down to sculpt, I trust myself to play and to express my true self. For me it is a very spiritual experience. The ability to imagine something and to make it real to be touched and shared is a joy.

Q. You often use symbols from nature in your work. Which symbols are you most drawn to in your bead designs and why?

A. I am drawn toward basic universal symbols. A tree, a house, a bird—they are all things most of us see in our daily life and they touch me as timeless. Sometimes I want to celebrate these simple beauties and sometimes I want to tell a story within my work. My most successful designs have been the result of pure playfulness.

Aphrodite's Charm Necklace

Hint sterling silver charm, Stephanie Ann lampworked disk

supplies

- 20 mm lampworked disk
- 12 mm silver shell charm
- **8** 10 mm chalcedony faceted coins
- **10** 8 mm rutilated quartz faceted rondelles
- **24** 3 mm apatite rondelles
- **16** 2 mm sterling silver beads or 11º seed beads
- **8** 11º green seed beads
- 38 mm silver leaf hook-and-eye clasp
- **5** 7 mm oval jump rings
- **40** 1-in. (2.5 cm) silver headpins
- 17 in. (43 cm) sterling silver oval chain cut into two equal lengths
- **2** 2-in. (5 cm) and one 4-in. (10 cm) lengths of 24-gauge sterling silver wire

finished length: 20 in. (51 cm)

basics

- wrapped bail
- plain loop
- wire-wrapped link

A

B

C

A Center the disk bead and the charm on a 4-in. length of wire and make a wire-wrapped bail.

B Make dangles: 24 apatite; eight 2 mm silver bead and quartz; eight seed bead, 2 mm silver bead, and chalcedony.

C On a 2-in. length of wire, create a wire-wrapped link with the quartz bead. Repeat. Attach the links to the chain ends with jump rings. Attach the clasp halves to the links with jump rings.

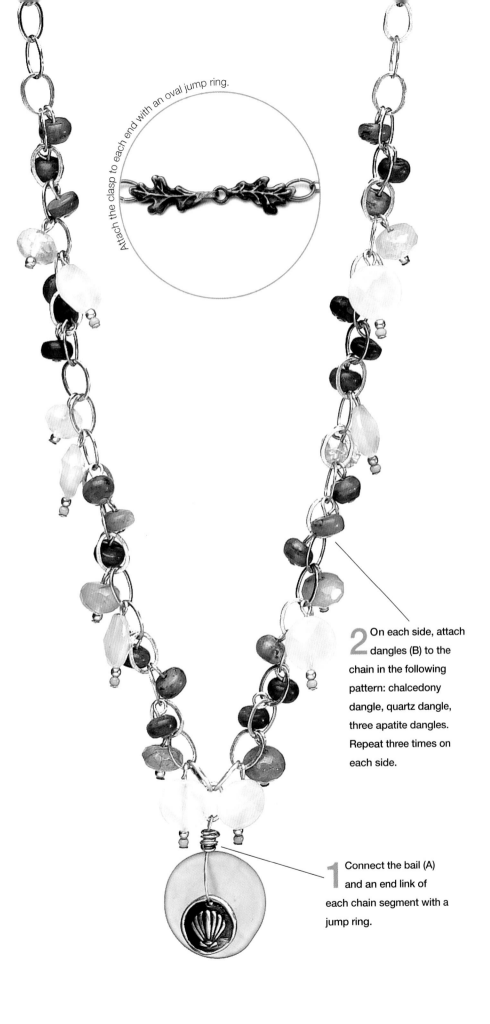

Attach the clasp to each end with an oval jump ring.

A delicate charm such as this seashell could easily get lost on a necklace. Create a stage for this little gem to shine by wire-wrapping a disk bead as the backdrop. Taking my cues from the faux sea glass disk, I paired watery shades of apatite and chalcedony with sand-colored quartz. The leaf-patterned clasp was reminiscent of seaweed to me and made a good match.

2 On each side, attach dangles (B) to the chain in the following pattern: chalcedony dangle, quartz dangle, three apatite dangles. Repeat three times on each side.

1 Connect the bail (A) and an end link of each chain segment with a jump ring.

Coral & Shell Necklace

Green Girl Studio pendants, Jubilee raku disks,
Earthenwood Studio shell charm

supplies

- 42 mm pewter shell pendant
- 25 mm pewter sun rock pendant
- 8 20–22 mm stick pearls
- 18 mm porcelain shell charm
- 12 15 mm raku disks
- 6 10 mm faceted recycled glass bead
- 8 6 mm rock crystal faceted rondelles
- 24 4 mm silver flat spacers
- 9 2 mm silver beads
- 3 1-in. (2.5 cm) silver headpins
- 2 5 mm gunmetal jump rings
- 6 in. (15 cm) gunmetal 10 mm oval chain plus seven extra chain links
- 26 in. (66 cm) 24-gauge sterling silver wire cut into six 4-in. (10 cm) lengths and one 2-in. (5 cm) length

finished length: 18 in. (46 cm)

basics

- wire-wrapped link
- opening and closing a jump ring

A

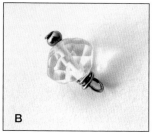

B

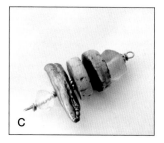

C

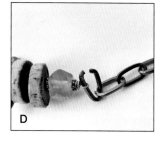

D

E

F

Components:

A Make a wire-wrapped link with a 20 mm stick pearl, attaching the shell charm to the bottom of loop before closing.

B Make a beaded dangle with a 2 mm silver bead and rock crystal. Make two.

C Make six wire-wrapped links using a rock crystal bead, a 2 mm bead, a pearl, a flat spacer, a raku bead, a flat spacer, a raku bead, a flat spacer, a glass bead, and a flat spacer.

D Open the end link on a 4-in. (10 cm) chain length and attach to a wrapped-loop end link. Repeat on the other side.

E On one side, open the end chain link and attach the pewter sun rock pendant.

F On a headpin, string a 2 mm bead and a pearl, and make a wrapped loop above the beads. Attach to one chain end.

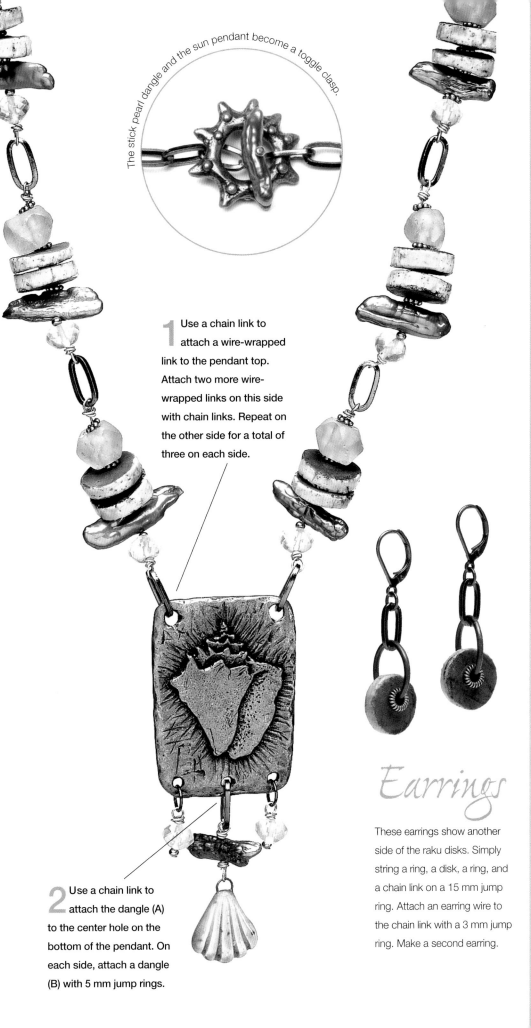

The stick pearl dangle and the sun pendant become a toggle clasp.

1 Use a chain link to attach a wire-wrapped link to the pendant top. Attach two more wire-wrapped links on this side with chain links. Repeat on the other side for a total of three on each side.

2 Use a chain link to attach the dangle (A) to the center hole on the bottom of the pendant. On each side, attach a dangle (B) with 5 mm jump rings.

This necklace is inspired by one of my favorite pastimes— beach combing. I love exploring the shore for hours searching for nature's tiniest treasures. Whether I'm looking for beach glass, hidden fossils, or shells, the sea-shore offers an endless inspiration of colors and textures. For the design of this piece, notice I used the links from the chain instead of jump rings, carrying the element throughout the necklace. The raku disk beads are paired with pearls, crystals, and recycled glass. Recycled glass resembles beach glass in its color and frosty tumbled appearance. The unique clasp is a pendant that has been transformed into a toggle with the help of a stick pearl.

Earrings

These earrings show another side of the raku disks. Simply string a ring, a disk, a ring, and a chain link on a 15 mm jump ring. Attach an earring wire to the chain link with a 3 mm jump ring. Make a second earring.

Sea Urchin Necklace

Humblebeads polymer clay urchin,
Heather Wynn polymer clay pendant,
Mamacita Beadworks pewter button,
Green Girl Studios pewter clasp

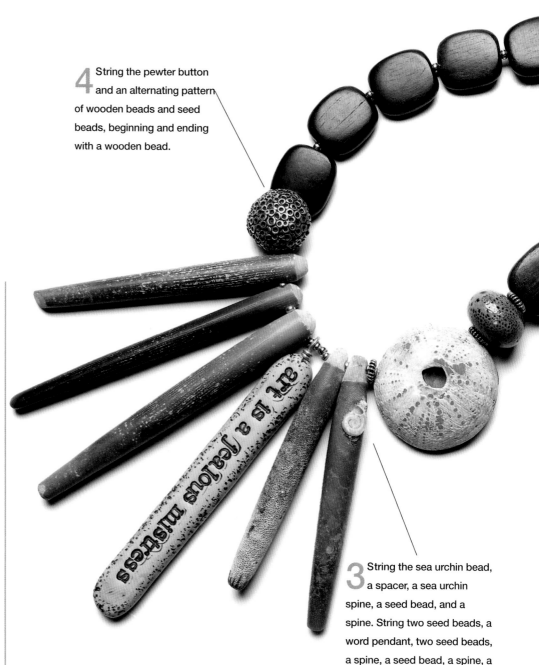

4 String the pewter button and an alternating pattern of wooden beads and seed beads, beginning and ending with a wooden bead.

3 String the sea urchin bead, a spacer, a sea urchin spine, a seed bead, and a spine. String two seed beads, a word pendant, two seed beads, a spine, a seed bead, a spine, a seed bead, and a spine.

supplies

- 30 mm polymer clay sea urchin
- polymer clay word pendant
- **5** sea urchin spine beads
- **16** 15 mm flat wooden beads
- 15 mm ceramic rondelle
- **2** 8 mm pink faceted glass beads
- **14** 8 mm peach keishi pearls
- **2** 6 mm bicone crystals
- **3** 6 mm flat silver spacers
- **43** nickel 11º seed beads
- pewter starfish toggle clasp
- 15 mm pewter button
- **2** crimp tubes
- 22 in. (56 cm) flexible beading wire

finished length: 18 in. (46 cm)

basics

- attaching a clasp
- crimping

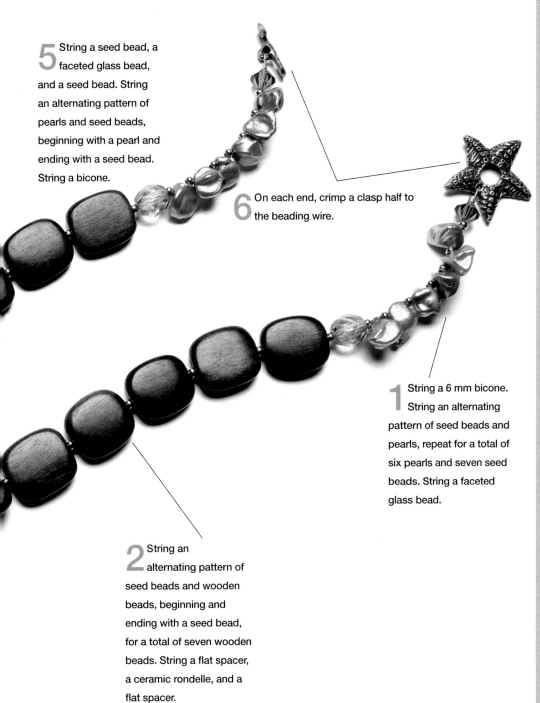

5 String a seed bead, a faceted glass bead, and a seed bead. String an alternating pattern of pearls and seed beads, beginning with a pearl and ending with a seed bead. String a bicone.

6 On each end, crimp a clasp half to the beading wire.

1 String a 6 mm bicone. String an alternating pattern of seed beads and pearls, repeat for a total of six pearls and seven seed beads. String a faceted glass bead.

2 String an alternating pattern of seed beads and wooden beads, beginning and ending with a seed bead, for a total of seven wooden beads. String a flat spacer, a ceramic rondelle, and a flat spacer.

Art and the sea are two jealous mistresses that find themselves entwined as the inspiration for this primitive necklace. A faux sea urchin and real sea-urchin spines pair perfectly in color and texture with a stamped polymer clay word pendant. The wooden beads are added as driftwood in this flotsam and jetsam collection.

Koi Pond Necklace

Sea of Glass lampworked focal,
Green Girl Studios clasp,
Kerri Fuhr Beads lampworked spacers

supplies

- 25 mm lampworked focal
- **4** 9–10 mm lampworked spacers
- **66** 8 mm African bloodstone rondelles
- **66** 11° nickel seed beads
- 6 mm silver flat spacer
- 45 mm gunmetal brass tassel
- 25 mm pewter fish toggle clasp
- **2** 2 mm silver crimp tubes
- 3 links of gunmetal chain
- 4 mm gunmetal jump ring
- 4 in. (10 cm) 20-gauge sterling silver wire
- flexible beading wire

finished length: 18 in. (46 cm)

basics

- wire-wrapped link
- attaching a clasp
- crimping

3 String an alternating pattern of stone beads and seed beads. Randomly substitute a lampworked spacer for a stone bead in two places on each side near the front.

4 Crimp the beading wire to an end chain link. Attach the fish toggle bar to the chain with a 4 mm jump ring.

2 Crimp the "water" to a length of beading wire.

1 Make a wire-wrapped link with a lampworked spacer, a focal bead, a 6 mm flat spacer, and a lampworked spacer. Connect the tassel to the bottom of the link loop and the "water" of the toggle pendant to the top of the link before the wraps are completed.

I don't know if the artist had fish in mind when she made this focal bead, but when I picked it up I knew instantly that it would be part of a koi pond creation. The color and pattern of the bead resemble scales. You can imagine my delight when I found this clasp that has a koi fish toggle bar swimming in its own pewter pond. Along with being a symbol of luck and prosperity, the koi symbolizes perseverance and strength. I picked stones to represent those qualities and that also naturally had the color of the focal bead. I added in a few lampworked spacers for more contrast. The lantern shape of the focal bead and tassel add to the feel of a garden pond.

Along the Reef Bracelet

SkullyB lampworked ruffles,
Mamacita Beadworks pewter,
Earthenwood Studio ceramics

supplies

- **4** 20 mm lampworked ruffle beads
- 15 mm ceramic disk
- 15 mm pewter button
- **8** 14 mm brown lava stone
- **2** 12 mm pewter bead caps
- **2** 10 mm wood rose beads
- **3** 8 mm faceted glass rondelles
- 8 mm faceted rutilated quartz round bead
- 6 mm faceted rutilated quartz rondelle
- 5 mm pearl
- 4 mm crystal bicone
- **9** nickel 11º seed beads
- **7** 4 mm flat spacers
- **2** 1-in. (2.5 cm) sterling silver headpins
- 6 in. (15 cm) 22-gauge half-hard sterling silver wire
- **2** 2 mm crimp tubes
- 12 in. flexible beading wire

basics

- make a hook clasp
- crimping
- attach a clasp
- wire-wrapped link
- wrapped loop

1 Make a hook clasp with 3 in. (7.6 cm) of 22-gauge wire. Crimp the hook clasp to the beading wire. Make a dangle with the crystal and wood rose and use a jump ring to attach it to the hook clasp.

2 String a quartz rondelle, a flat spacer, a lava stone, two seed beads, a lava stone, a flat spacer, a wooden bead, a flat spacer, a lava stone, two seed beads, a lava stone, and bead cap.

A

Clasp half:

A Make a wire-wrapped link using 3 in. of 22-gauge wire and the button. Make one loop slightly larger than the other.

Make dangles:
- a seed bead and a pearl
- a flat spacer and a crystal

Use a jump ring to connect the pearl and crystal dangles to the small loop of the button link.

5 Crimp the small loop of the button link to the wire.

3 String a lampworked ruffle and a crystal rondelle. Repeat twice. String a ruffle bead and a bead cap.

4 String a lava stone, a flat spacer, a wood rose, a flat spacer, a lava bead, two seed beads, a lava stone, two seed beads, a lava stone, a flat spacer, and a quartz bead.

The lava stone beads remind me of the coast along Cozumel, where I went snorkeling for the first time. I was so amazed by the life beneath the waves; it was an ebb and flow of fish, coral, and plants dancing along to the rhythm of the ocean. I chose to pair the lava stone with a fluttering set of lampworked ruffle beads that reminded me of that underwater adventure. This bracelet is all about the mix of textures, pairing the rough, matte lava with the smooth, shiny glass. Creating a clasp out of a button adds a fun twist to the traditional hook-and-eye clasp and sneaks in another opportunity to play up the tactile fun of this design.

Earrings

Sometimes a pretty bead and a simple wire bail is all you need for earrings. These beads are from Sea of Glass and each bail is made with 3 in. (7.6 cm) of 20-gauge silver wire.

Basics

Plain Loop

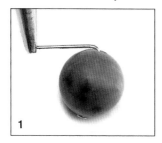

1

2

3

4

1 Trim the wire ⅜ in. (1 cm) above the top bead. Make a right-angle bend close to the bead.

2 Grab the wire's tip with roundnose pliers. Roll the wire to form a half circle.

3 Reposition the pliers in the loop and continue rolling, forming a centered circle above the bead.

4 The finished loop.

To make a beaded loop link, use a 2-in. (5 cm) piece of wire. Make a plain loop at one end. Slide a bead on the wire and make a second plain loop at the end.

Wrapped Loop

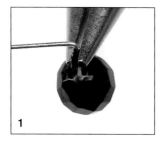

1

2

3

4

1 Make sure there is at least 1¼ in. (3.2 cm) of wire above the bead. With the tip of your chainnose pliers, grasp the wire directly above the bead. Bend the wire (above the pliers) into a right angle.

2 Position the jaws of your roundnose pliers vertically in the bend.

3 Bring the wire over the pliers' top jaw.

4 Reposition the pliers' lower jaw snugly in the curved wire. Wrap the wire down and around the bottom of the pliers. This is the first half of a wrapped loop.

5

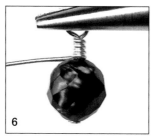

6

5 Grasp the loop with chainnose pliers.

6 Wrap the wire tail around the wire stem, covering the stem between the loop and the top

bead. Trim the excess wrapping wire, and press the end close to the stem with chainnose or crimping pliers.

To make a beaded wrapped-loop link, use a 3½-in. (8.9 cm) piece of wire. Make a wrapped loop at one end. Slide a bead on the wire and make a second wrapped loop at the end.

Opening a Jump Ring or Loop

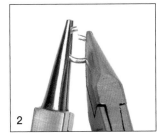

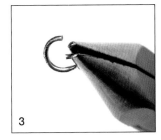

1 Hold the jump ring or loop with chainnose and roundnose pliers or two pairs of chain-nose pliers.

2 To open the jump ring or loop, bring one pair of pliers toward you.

3 The open jump ring. Reverse the steps to close.

Folded Crimp

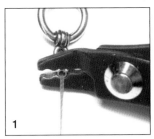

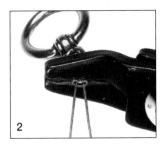

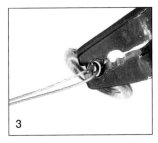

1 Position the crimp bead in the notch closest to the crimping pliers' handle.

2 Separate the wires and firmly squeeze the crimp bead.

3 Move the crimp bead into the notch at the pliers' tip. Squeeze the pliers, folding the bead in half at the indentation.

4 The folded crimp.

Attaching a Clasp

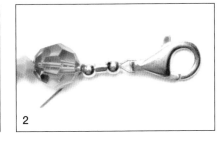

1 For a two-piece clasp, on each end, string: spacer, crimp bead, spacer, Wire Guardian (optional), and half of a clasp. Check the fit, and add or remove beads if necessary. Go back through the beads just strung and tighten the wire. Crimp the crimp bead and trim the excess wire.

2 Alternately, attach a lobster claw clasp on one end and a soldered jump ring or chain extender on the other.

Basics

Wrapped Bail

1 Insert a ball headpin through disk bead and create a loop with the end of the wire.

2 Wrap the ball part of the headpin around the loop.

3 Continue wrapping the rest of the wire around the loop. Push the ball closer to the loop with chainnose pliers if needed.

Entwined Loop

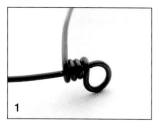

1 Make a wrapped loop with four wraps.

2 Continue wrapping the wire around the loop, pushing the wire with your finger. Cross the wire up and down several times to create the entwined texture.

3 Trim the wire and flatten the end with chainnose pliers.

4 The finished entwined loop.

Note: Use 3–5 in. of extra wire, depending on how large you want the wrapped portion.

To make an entwined loop link, use 10 in. (25 cm) of wire. Make an entwined loop at one end. Slide a bead on the wire and make an entwined loop at the end, wrapping the wire in a similar fashion to the wraps you made in step 2.

Wire Tendrils

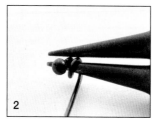

1 Wrap a ball headpin around the tip of roundnose pliers.

2 Continue wrapping 2–3 more times.

3 Use chainnose pliers to pull the wire and center the tendrils.

Make a Hook-and-Eye Clasp

1

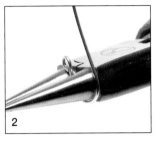

3

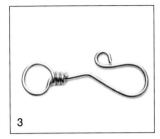

4

1 Cut a 3-in. (7.6 cm) length of wire. Turn a small loop at one end.

2 Grasp the base of the loop near the base of roundnose pliers' jaws.

3 Bend the wire around the jaw in the opposite direction of the loop. Use chainnose pliers to make a small bend at the end of the hook, roughly lined up with the small loop.

Make a large wrapped loop at the end of the wire.

4 Cut a 3-in. length of wire. Make a large wrapped loop at one end.

Gently hammer the hook and eye shapes to strengthen and flatten the wire.

To attach a necklace, make the first half of a wrapped loop at the other end of the eye wire and attach it to chain. Or, finish the wraps and crimp a beaded strand to the loop.

Check the Fit

Before you attach the clasp, tape each wire end and check the fit of the necklace. If necessary, remove the tape and add or remove beads from each side.

Cutting Flexible Beading Wire

Decide how long you'd like your necklace to be. Add 6 in. (15 cm) and cut a piece of beading wire to that length. (For a bracelet, add 5 in./13 cm.)

About the Author

Heather Powers is an innovative bead and jewelry artist. Her art beads are collected by enthusiasts around the world. Her work has been featured on television, in magazines, and in books. Her main ambition in life is to help inspire others to create. Heather graduated from Kendall College of Art and Design with a Bachelor of Arts degree in fine arts. It was during art school that she first discovered beads and soon became obsessed, translating her color and design skills into jewelry and beads. Along with being a busy designer, Heather is also the founder and editor of the Art Bead Scene, an interactive blog that celebrates art beads and inspires those who use them. She also organizes an annual bead cruise, teaching classes and offering inspiration while enjoying beaches and tropical breezes. She lives in San Antonio where she is a work-at-home mom, balancing business and family. Occasionally you'll find her drawing, writing, and illustrating for the children's book market and even more occasionally, you'll find her sleeping! You can always find her online at humblebeads.com.

My jewelry is more than just adding a bead to a string; each piece speaks to me of the wonders of the world.

Acknowledgments

This book is dedicated to my family: Without your love and support I wouldn't be able to create and enjoy this bead-filled life!

Thank you to my mom for being my biggest cheerleader. I couldn't have written this book without her. Thank you for being my biggest fan and dearest friend.

Thanks to my dad for showing me the beauty of nature when I was a child and for teaching me to take the path less traveled.

Thank you to my husband Jess. I couldn't do all of this without his support. And thank you to my daughters, Hannah and Evangeline, for allowing me time to create and valuing my work. Thanks to my aunt Rosanne for all her bead-related support!

Thank you to my friends in the bead world. They are a constant source of inspiration and encouragement. I would especially like to thank my friend Erin for all of her support and friendship over the last few years. Thank you to my Art Bead Scene editors for helping to build an incredible community and to our readers who support us each day.

Thank you to the beadmakers and suppliers who donated items for the book. There are too many to mention; please know that I am thankful for all of you!

Thank you to Mary Wohlgemuth for encouraging me to submit this book. And lastly, I offer my deepest thanks to Karin Van Voorhees for her patience while I worked up the courage to finally send in the proposal and for her guidance and support during the writing process.

Sources

(Sources listed in project order)

Evergreen Bracelet and Earrings
Toggle: Mary Harding. Pewter owl: Green Girl Studios. Stick pearls: Fire Mountain Gems and Beads. Stones: Rings & Things. Disk beads: Humblebeads. Bead caps: Ornamentea.

Nurture Thy Soul Necklace
Patina chain, wire, and ball headpins: Miss Fickle Media. Bird nest toggle: Humblebeads. Lampworked double-dipped headpin: Cindy Gimbrone Beads. Silver bird bead: Elemental Adornments.

Out on a Limb Necklace
Leaf-fringe chain: Lima Beads. Copper chain: Michaels. Bead caps and flower clasp: Beading House. Copper and resin branch components: Jade Scott. Pewter beads: Green Girl Studios. Polymer clay beads: Humblebeads.

Birch Forest Bracelet
Lampworked beads: Sue Beads. Nickel seed beads: Charlene's Beads.

The Sweetest Song Necklace
Painted brass leaf: Paloma Antiqua. Ceramic leaf, find a similar design by Chinook Jewelry. Bird pendant and nest bead: Green Girl Studios. Ceramic rounds: Elaine Ray. Houses: Jubilee. Egg and disks: Humblebeads. Clasp: C-Koop. Brass filigree: Vintaj Natural Brass Co.

Above the Tree Tops Necklace
Clasp: Green Girl Studios. Peanut seed beads: Fusion Beads. Disk beads: Humblebeads. Copper seed beads: Charlene's Beads. Beadcaps and melon beads: Beading House.

Be True Necklace
Polymer clay pendant: Heather Wynn. Pewter charm and bird: Green Girl Studios. Brass clasp, filigree, and charms: Vintaj Natural Brass Co. Seed beads: Charlene's Beads.

Three Sisters Necklace
Polymer clay pendant: Block Party Press. Leaf clasp: Shipwreck Beads. Connectors: Rings & Things.

Autumn Lariat
Lampworked Acorns: Credit River Art Glass. Ruffle lampworked beads: SkullyB Beads, find a similar design at Modern Trails. Filigree cones: Vintaj Natural Brass Co. Variation: Lampworked beads: Dora Schubert. Bead caps: Ornamentea. Brass leaves: Vintaj Natural Brass Co.

Winter Solstice Necklace
Pewter pendant: Lynn Davis. Stones: Rings & Things. Clasp: Ornamentea

Oh Nuts Necklace
Squirrel and acorn beads: Diane Hawkey. Disk bead and acorn charm: Earthenwood. Acorn pendant: Gaea ceramic. Copper and resin acorn pendant: Jade Scott. Chain: Ornamentea. Long headpins: Michael's Industrial Chic.

Leaving Home Bracelet
Word bead: Diane Hawkey. House bead: Jubilee. Lampworked beads: Cindy Craig. Clasp: Green Girl Studios. Wooden beads: Hobby Lobby.

Daffodil Fields Necklace
Silver bead: Anne Choi. Glass beads: Stephanie Anne. Stones: Rings & Things.

Titania's Bower Necklace
Ceramic flower: seaurchin. Elaine Ray ceramic beads: Ornamentea. Other ceramic beads: Gaea. Lampworked headpins: Lampwork Diva. Lampworked beads: Sue Beads. Brass bead caps, pendant, and jump ring: Vintaj Natural Brass Co. Copper seed beads: Charlene's Beads. Chain: Hobby Lobby.

Medieval Medallion Necklace
Polymer clay bead: Gabriel. Filigree: Vintaj Natural Brass Co.

Flight of the Bumblebee Bracelet
Lampworked beads: Kerri Fuhr. Peanut seed beads: Fusion Beads. Clasp: Green Girl Studios. Brass Charm: Vintaj Natural Brass Co. Stones: Rings & Things.

Zen Garden Bracelet
Polymer clay beads: Humblebeads. Stones and pearls: Rings & Things. Lampworked disks: Blue Seraphim. Nickel seed beads: Charlene's Beads.

Garden Gate Earrings
Polymer clay beads: Lynn Davis.

Thistles & Blooms Bracelet
Ceramic pendant and connector: Chinook Jewelry. Clasp and bead cap: Holly Gage. Lampworked beads: Cindy Hoo. Pewter button: Mamacita Beadworks.

Dragonfly Pond Necklace
Glass rings: Sea of Glass. Polymer clay: Humblebeads. Resin: Natural Touch Beads. Dragonflies: Vintaj Natural Brass Co.

Forget Me Knot Necklace
Ceramic Pendant: Lisa Peters Art. Teardrop: Miss Fickle Media. Chain, bead caps, and rhinestone bead: Ornamentea.

Effervescence Necklace
Pewter pendant: Mamacita Beadworks. Lampworked headpins: Kelley's Beads. Lampworked disks: HMB Studios. Round chain: Hobby Lobby. Cable chain: Ornamentea.

Into the Deep Necklace
Polymer clay beads: Pam Wynn. Lampworked ruffles: Starlia Phillips. Ceramic round bead: Elaine Ray. Faceted ceramic beads: Diane Hawkey. Glass seashells and rugged coins: Sonoran Beads. Rhinestone beads: Ornamentea. Clasp: Green Girl Studios. Etched jump rings: Vintaj Natural Brass Co.

Bronze Nautilus Earrings
Polymer clay beads: Miss Fickle Media. Pearls: Rings & Things.

Caribbean Waters Bracelet
Glass rings: Cindy Gimbrone. Glass bead: Sue Beads. Filigree rings, jump rings, hammered ring and toggle bar: Vintaj Natural Brass Co. Brass rings: Michaels.

Jellyfish Necklace
Glass beads: Stephanie Ann. Chain: Ornamentea. Starfish: Vintaj Natural Brass Co. Fluorite beads: Rings & Things. Large brass headpin: Michaels.

Tide Pool Treasures Bracelet
Starfish bead: Stephanie Ann. Coconut beads: Hobby Lobby. Variation: Lampworked bead: Blue Seraphim. Chain: Hobby Lobby.

Aphrodite's Charm Necklace
Silver charm: Hint. Lampworked disk: Stephanie Ann. Stones: Rings & Things. Clasp: Shipwreck Beads.

Coral & Shell Necklace
Pewter pendants: Green Girl Studios. Shell charm: Earthenwood Studio. Raku disk beads: Jubilee. Recycled glass: Natural Touch Beads. Chain, pearls, and stones: Rings & Things.

Sea Urchin Necklace
Polymer clay urchin: Humblebeads. Polymer clay pendant: Heather Wynn. Sea urchin spines and keishi pearls: Rings & Things. Pewter clasp: Green Girl Studios. Wooden beads: Hobby Lobby.

Koi Pond Necklace
Lampworked focal: Sea of Glass. Lampworked spacers: Kerri Fuhr. Toggle clasp: Green Girl Studios. Tassel: Rings & Things. Stones: Cherry Tree Beads.

Along the Reef Bracelet
Lampworked beads: Skully B Beads, find a similar design at Modern Trails. Pewter: Mamacita Beadworks. Ceramic: Earthenwood. Lava stone beads: Rings & Things.

Source Websites
Anne Choi: annechoi.com
Beading House: beadinghouse.com
Block Party Press:
  blockpartypress.etsy.com
Blue Seraphim: blueseraphim.etsy.com
Charlene's Beads: cbbeads.com
Cherry Tree Beads: cherrytreeebeads.com
Chinook Jewelry: chinookjewelry.com
Cindy Craig: artglassadornments.com
Cindy Gimbrone Beads:
  cindygimbronebeads.com
Cindy Hoo: cindyhoo.etsy.com
C-Koop: ckoopbeads.com
Credit River Art Glass: creditriverartglass.com
Diane Hawkey: fusionbeads.com
Dora Schubert: doraschubert.com
Earthenwood Studio:
  earthenwoodstudio.com
Elaine Ray: ornamentea.com
Elemental Adornments:
  elementaladornments.com
Fire Mountain Gems and Beads:
  firemountaingems.com
Fusion Beads: fusionbeads.com
Gabriel: gabriel.etsy.com
Gaea: gaea.cc
Green Girl Studios: greengirlstudios.com
Heather Wynn: swoondimples.etsy.com
HMB Studios: hmbstudios.etsy.com
Hint: hint.etsy.com
Hobby Lobby: hobbylobby.com
Holly Gage: hollygage.com
Humblebeads: humblebeads.com
Jade Scott: jadescott.etsy.com
Jubilee: jubilee.etsy.com
Kelley's Beads: kelleysbeads.etsy.com
Kerri Fuhr: kerrifuhr.com
Lampwork Diva: cindygimbronebeads.com
Lima Beads: limabeads.com
Lisa Peters Art: lisapetersart.com
Lynn Davis: lynndavis.etsy.com
Mamacita Beadworks:
  mamacitabeadworks.com
Mary Harding: maryhardingjewelry.com
Modern Trails: moderntrails.etsy.com
Michaels: michaels.com
Miss Fickle Media: missficklemedia.etsy.com
Natural Touch Beads:
  naturaltouchbeads.com
Ornamentea: ornamentea.com
Paloma Antigua: palomaantigua.etsy.com
Pam Wynn: pamwynn.etsy.com
Rings & Things: rings-things.com
Sea of Glass: mjrbeads.com
seaurchin: seaurchin.etsy.com
Shipwreck Beads: shipwreckbeads.com
SkullyB Beads: find similar beads at
  moderntrails.etsy.com
Sonoran Beads: sonoranbeads.com
Starlia Phillips: starliaphillips.com
Stephanie Ann: stephaniebeads.com
Sue Beads: suebeads.etsy.com
Vintaj Natural Brass Co.: Vintaj.com

Art Beads on Inspiration Pages Made By:
Page 14: Copper Tree: Jennifer Stumpf. Ceramic Nest: Shandra Lee. Polymer Clay Oak Leaf: Humblebeads. Polymer Clay Wood Grain: Block Party Press. Ceramic Pine Cone: Mary Harding. Glass Pine Cone Beads: Kim Fields. Ceramic Acorn: Diane Hawkey. Polymer Clay Acorn: Humblebeads.
Page 15: Glass Egg: Kelley's Beads. Polymer Clay Bird: Humblebeads. Polymer Clay Word Pendant and Bird Charm: Heather Wynn. Pewter Owl and Nest: Green Girl Studios. Ceramic Owl and Bird Pendant: Spirited Earth. Ceramic Leaf and Disks: Earthenwood Studio. Ceramic Leaf: Gaea. **Page 42:** Glass Gingko: Lisa Kan. Ceramic Flower: Chinook Jewelry. Pewter Lotus: Green Girl Studios. Pewter Flower Button: Mamacita Beadworks. Ceramic Bee: Gaea. Glass Beads: Sue Beads. Ceramic Leaf Bead: Joan Miller Porcelain. Polymer Clay Tigerlily Bead: Humblebeads. **Page 43:** Glass Lavender Bead: LavenderBeads. Ceramic Leaf: Lisa Peters. Glass Flower Bead: Kim Fields. Ceramic Bead: Earthenwood Studio. Pewter Snail: Green Girl Studios. **Page 64:** Glass Disks: Blue Seraphim. Ceramic Shell: Gaea. Pewter Anchor: Lynn Davis. Glass Skeleton Key: The Venerable Bead. Ceramic Button Trio: Lisa Peteres. **Page 65:** Ceramic Starfish: Joan Miller Porcelain. Green Ceramic Bead: Elaine Ray. Glass Disks: Stephanie Ann. Ceramic Sand Dollar: Earthenwood Studio. Polymer Clay Urchin: Humblebeads. Pewter Button: Miss Fickle Media. Glass Disks: SkullyB. Pewter Starfish: Green Girl Studios. Ceramic Fish: Summers Studio. Ceramic Sand Dollar: Erin Siegel.

Visit Heather's website (humblebeads.com) for links to these artists.